Preparing a
Business
Plan

Tony Compton

Wrightbooks

Also by TONY COMPTON, published by and available from Wrightbooks:

Trading With a Plan
Rental Property and Taxation
Shares, Derivatives and Taxation
Buying a Small Business

ACKNOWLEDGMENT: The author and publisher would like to thank the FMRC Benchmarking Team for allowing the use of their material in this book.

Wrightbooks Pty Ltd   Ph: (03) 9532 7082
PO Box 270   Fax: (03) 9532 7084
Elsternwick   E-mail: info@wrightbooks.com.au
Victoria   3185   Website: www.wrightbooks.com.au

First published by Wrightbooks in 1999. Reprinted March 2001.

National Library of Australia Cataloguing-in-Publication data:

Compton, Tony, 1951-.

Preparing a business plan.

Bibliography.

Includes index.

ISBN 1 876627 10 7.

1. New business enterprises - Planning. 2. Business planning.

658.4012

Cover design by Rob Cowpe
Printed in Australia by McPherson's Printing Group
ISBN: 1 876627 10 7

NOTE

CONTENTS

PREFACE

"IF YOU FAIL TO PLAN... you are planning to fail" the header shouted at me from the document in my fax machine. The unsolicited mailer from a firm of management consultants was offering a free report titled '*Business Planning... what it is and what's in it for you.*' I put it to the side, not really having any interest. My experience was that business plans didn't work. That feeling was supported by statistics which showed that the existence of a business plan did not seem to be a significant factor in the failure rates of small business. The reason was obvious. Business plans were normally prepared at the request of a lending institution to support an application for finance. Often the owners had little input into the plan and paid a substantial sum of money to a management consultant for its preparation. After it had done its job (assisted in raising funds) the plan was filed away, never to surface again. Why? Probably because it was not understood by the business owner, and if it was the relevance escaped him.

For that reason I had some doubts when asked if I would be interested in writing this book. Why expend energy writing about preparing a document which would be used once, then cast away to gather dust? After a little thought I changed my mind. That is not what business plans should be about. They should not be documents prepared with the sole purpose of assisting with an application for finance. Sure, they could be submitted along with

v

an application, but they should be more than that. They have a far more important use.

A business plan should be a dynamic ongoing document, its preparation requiring a continuing involvement from the business owner. He should be the person setting the goals, adjusting targets, making changes as events unfold and ensuring the business does not stray from the path laid down. The plan should be his, not someone else's.

Business planning is clearly not about writing a boring application for finance, setting out, amongst other things, the name and address of the business, who its owners are, and who its bankers and advisers are. The business owner already knows that. If necessary, such a sheet can be attached to a plan when submitting it to a financier. A business plan should not be about supplying historical data as to the past performance of a business. It should not be about setting out cash flow forecasts that have been prepared because the bank wants them and for no other reason. It should not be about the preparation of pages of figures based on fantasy. Business planning should be about preparing a blueprint for the future, a map and a realistic guide for the journey that a business has yet to complete and part of what Michael Gerber of "The E-Myth" fame refers to when he pleads for people to spend more time working *on* their business rather than working *in* it.

So I pulled out the fax and read it again. It claimed, "93% of successful businesses have a fully researched and written business plan and almost all business failures don't." This conflicts with a finding in a study by A.J. Williams, from the University of Newcastle, in 1987. He found that of the 9.4% of small businesses in Australia which had a business plan, 48% failed – compared to a 54.4% failure rate of firms that either did not plan or rarely or poorly planned. And it was at odds with my experience of the many successful businesses that I have as clients (who do not have a business plan). Further, it is not supported by the Australian Bureau of Statistics (ABS) figures I had seen. These (from the ABS

publication *Characteristics of Small Business Australia 1997*)
revealed that only 18.4% of small businesses had a business plan,
and that 10.5% of small businesses with a plan did not operate
under the plan. Only 15.2% of small businesses with less than five
employees had a plan. Far more than this number operate
successfully, so where did the 93% figure come from?

According to the fax, the 93% was the "result of two recent surveys,
one by a Queensland government department." That really interested
me. After all, a survey by a Queensland government department
would get it right. Wouldn't it? I was sceptical, to say the least, but
my curiosity aroused, I decided to fax back the coupon at the
bottom of the flier saying "Yes. I'd like to know more about Business
Planning for Success." At worst, I reasoned, I would find out what
the survey was, and who was surveyed. None of my clients were,
but that didn't surprise me, because my practice is small and
statistically insignificant in the scheme of things. Neither were the
clients of any of the accountants I knew. Or at least we were
unaware of anyone being surveyed. I awaited the report with
interest. It never arrived. I didn't follow it up, as I doubted that
there was anything new that it would say which would have been
of use to me. I may have been terribly wrong, but I will never
know.

Tony Compton
Brisbane
October 1999

WHERE TO START

THE HARDEST PART of doing something unfamiliar is knowing where to start and understanding why you are doing it. If you are only preparing a business plan because your bank wants you to, don't waste your time. The bank doesn't need it, but you do. Most times, all the bank needs is your latest financial statements, and perhaps a cash flow statement to show what your anticipated needs are and your ability to service the debt. So forget the traditional plan. Its preparation may assist in obtaining a loan, but if your business is strong, you will get the loan without one.

Instead, prepare a plan you can use – one that is meaningful and helps with the management of your business. Give that to the bank if it insists on a plan. Remember the bank is only interested in selling to you. It does not provide a service. Banks sell the commodity of money. If your business is strong and healthy they are not going to pass up the chance of making a profit from you just because you don't have a business plan. And they won't lend to you if you don't fulfil their lending criteria, no matter how well prepared or fancy a plan you submit to them. So if you are going to prepare a plan, prepare one that is of use to you, not them.

Don't get me wrong. I am not saying don't plan. On the contrary, I believe that all business owners should plan. This does not necessarily have to be in a written form – but they should have goals and a vision as to where they are heading. What I am saying is, don't prepare a traditional business plan unless it is going to be useful to you. For me a successful plan is one that is dog-eared, tattered, full of comments added later and revised. In short – one that is used as an ongoing management tool, and referred to often. Few of these exist.

ASK YOURSELF SOME QUESTIONS

Knowing where to start involves knowing why the plan is being prepared. Without a map for the future a business will trade from day to day without any real purpose. It may be profitable and it may grow, but it would do so as a result of circumstance rather than good management. To prepare the map, you need to know where you are going and why. That is why you should plan. So how do you start? That is easy. Just ask yourself this question:

What will my business look like when I am finished with it?

Most of us will have difficulty with that. Some will say, "How can I know? I don't have a crystal ball!", so to help answer that question ask yourself another:

What do I want to be doing with myself when I am finished with my business?

Then ask:

How can my business help me achieve that?

All this is leading to the identification of your goals. It is an articulation of what your business is about and why it is there. This should be the beginning of the business plan because the plan should be about setting out the means of achieving the goals of the business owner.

MISSION STATEMENTS

Some businesses attempt to articulate their goals through a mission statement. A mission statement is a summary of the purpose of a business and how that purpose will be achieved. It expresses what a business is set up to do and how it aims to do it. Many I have seen are nothing more than a series of slick words setting out lofty goals which are seldom related to the way the business really works. They are prepared because it is 'the thing to do', a way of attempting to express what some call a business's unique selling proposition. The latest business guru tells management to prepare one so they do, because they believe that if they don't, they will be seen to be inefficient and not keeping up with the times.

If you do want to prepare a mission statement, make it meaningful. Not only should it express what your organisation is attempting to achieve, it should express what your organisation actually does. A statement that includes the words: "It is our purpose to not only satisfy our customers but to absolutely delight them", will be meaningless if the organisation espousing it is known to provide an inferior service or product. More so, it is probably dishonest. The real purpose of such a statement is probably to create as much wealth (ethically or otherwise) for the organisation and its owners as possible.

Perhaps, if you prepare one, the mission statement should be for your eyes and those of your staff only. The customers don't need to know your goals or what you are attempting to achieve. You and your employees do. An in-house mission statement may well make for a more honest one. After all, most people are in business to make a profit. They are pretending if they say they are there to provide for the wellbeing of the community that they serve.

I once had a client who believed his business was there to provide employment for his employees. He could see no point in making profits and then paying large amounts of tax. So he ran his business to make a living and provide jobs. Whilst admiring his social conscience, his partner thought otherwise. The business no longer exists. The partner could see financial problems looming and ended the relationship. Much bitterness ensued, but the reality was that the owners were risking their assets to maintain jobs in a business that was barely breaking even. A disaster was ahead and was narrowly avoided. The reality is that most small business owners are in business to create wealth. If they are there for any other reason then they don't have a business, they have a job, or a pastime.

So whether it be a mission statement or a summary of what you do and how you do it, make it honest. But prepare it. It is the basis for your plan. (See page 14 for more information.)

 LET'S PREPARE A BUSINESS PLAN

The basic principles underlying the preparation of the type of plan I am referring to hold no matter what sort of business is being considered. So let's look at a plan prepared by the fictional character of James (Jim) Watson. James is 35 years of age, married with no children and no plans to have any. He and his wife own and operate a specialty car repair and suspension parts wholesale centre from Springwood, a suburb of Logan City, Queensland, and coincidently where my accountancy practice is located.

Jim is concerned that his business, whilst profitable, is going nowhere. He has goals and realises that if he doesn't begin to plan time will pass him by before they have been achieved. Jim and his wife, Marney, come to me to talk about their future in business. They are concerned that they are spending long hours in their business and, in their eyes, barely making a living.

"What do we do?" Jim asks, his blank look broadcasting his current state of depression. "The figures show that we are making money but I don't know where it is going, and I feel that I am getting nowhere."

This comment was nothing new to me. I had heard it many times before. Jim was so busy working his business that he had no time to think about where he wanted it to go.

"I start at the shop at 8 in the morning and don't get home till 6 at night. On Saturdays, I finish at 4, and Sundays are our day off."

I listened, feeling sorry for my client. I had known him since he started the workshop five years ago, and had seen him develop the business from nothing to where it was now providing, as far as I could see, a good living.

"You own your own home, don't you?" I asked.

"Sure," Jim answered, his American twang betraying a childhood spent in the Everglades of Florida.

"How did you pay for it?" I asked, knowing the answer.

"From the business," he replied.

Jim had few funds of his own when he commenced in business. He borrowed to pay for the stock he needed, using guarantees provided by his parents to obtain the finance. That loan was still outstanding but he had repaid a $100,000 loan which he had obtained to buy a modest three-bedroom home in Rochedale, an adjoining suburb to Springwood. He had paid his taxes along the way, and to me he had been successful. Yet here he was sitting in my office, having saved sufficient funds to buy a home in five years, feeling that he was going nowhere.

I reminded him of this. Marney smiled, knowing only too well that they were doing fine. "We don't know where we are going," she said. "I don't think we want to be behind the counter in another five years' time, and we are tired. We need a holiday."

"Have you prepared a plan?" I asked.

"You mean a business plan?" Jim asked in return.

"Yes," I replied.

"No," was the predictable answer. "But why should I do that? I don't want to borrow money, and the people I have spoken to in the local Chamber of Commerce, who have, say they were a waste of time."

"They needn't be," I said, and proceeded to explain the reasons for planning and how the plan I was talking about was different to those traditionally prepared.

"But I haven't the time," Jim said, offering a normal excuse, "and they cost the earth."

I smiled, recalling the business development seminars I had attended which espoused the benefits of accountants getting out of compliance work and into the lucrative field of business planning where fees of $3,500 per day, so it was said, are achievable.

"Not necessarily," I countered. "Not if you do most of the work."

"But I don't know where to start," Jim said, Marney nodding in agreement.

"Let me show you," I replied. I turned to the filing cabinet behind my desk, and took out a file marked 'Business Development Questionnaire'. I had obtained this from a seminar I attended some years back, and had rarely used it. I pulled out a copy of the questionnaire and handed the first sheet to Jim. "But first, take this away and answer the questions. Bring it back next week and we will go through it. There are only four questions, and we need a place to start. In the meantime I will crunch a few numbers here, and we will talk about them along with what you bring back to me. We will need about a month to get the job done."

"What will it cost?" they asked in unison, concerned about the likely accounting fees.

"What might it cost if you don't do it?" I replied, turning the question back onto them.

"Let's start off by agreeing that if you don't get a benefit from what we are about to do, you won't pay me anything," I offered. I had never done this before, but I liked my clients and saw a challenge ahead. I had heard of this technique as a way to get new business, but was not using it for that purpose. I wanted Jim and Marney to feel that the risk of preparing the plan was being removed and I knew they needed the work done.

"It will probably cost around $2,000 for starters, but that could increase significantly from the monitoring work that might follow." I hated quoting. I have never been good at estimating time, and unlike some of my colleagues I felt morally obliged to honour any estimate provided.

"What will we get for the $2,000?" was Marney's next question.

"A blueprint for your future," I answered. "A business plan that will be different enough from the conventional idea to be useful to you, and one which you will understand, because you will have prepared most of it yourself."

"Why are we going to pay you $2,000 then?" Jim asked.

"Because you need me to show you the way," I answered, reminding him that he was the one asking for help, not me.

"Okay," he agreed. "We need to do something."

I felt comfortable about the $2,000. They would get far more value than that out of what they were going to do, and I had based the fee on an estimated 15 hours of work, a far cry from the $3,500 a day some of my colleagues were earning. I knew there was little risk in them not paying, and the likelihood of follow-on work was probable.

They left after making a time to see me the next week, the questionnaire in hand, both feeling that they might have taken the first step in reviving their feelings for their business.

KEY POINTS

- ☛ A business plan should be an ongoing and evolving business tool.

- ☛ It should be referred to often and, in the main, be prepared by the business owner(s).

- ☛ The plan should be looked upon as a map to help get the business from where it is now to where the business owner wants it to be in the future.

2

ESTABLISHING WHERE YOU WANT THE BUSINESS TO BE

CASE STUDY   KNOWING YOUR GOALS

Sunday was usually a lazy day in the Watson household, a day spent recovering from the long hours in the workshop, and relaxing. But not this Sunday. After an early breakfast the sheet I had given them was placed on the table. Pencil in hand, Jim and Marney began to go through the questions.

The first one took them aback.

Question 1: What do you want to be doing in five years' time?

"What has that got to do with running a repair centre?" Marney asked.

"I don't know," replied Jim, "but let's answer it anyway."

"I want to be lying on the beach at Noosa, enjoying the warm winter sun, watching all the girls go by," Jim said, reeling back as Marney aimed a gentle punch at his arm.

"Get real!" Marney exlaimed in her typical North Queensland drawl. "You're 35 years old, none of them would look back at you!" Marney had grown up in Cairns and had not lost the accent common to that region.

"Let's think about it," they both said at the same time.

"I don't want to be in the shop," Jim said emphatically.

"What would you do without it?" Marney asked.

"I have no idea, but I don't want to be behind the service counter," was Jim's response.

"Well, we will be too young to retire, and I like being in business," Marney said. "Maybe we should be working, but working in a different way. I think I would like to be managing the business rather than running it."

"But that isn't possible at Springwood," said Jim.

"You yanks can't think past your nose! What if we had three centres?"

"I haven't thought about that, I've been too busy working the business to think about developing it. Maybe you have something there."

"Holidays, weekends, the theatre, golf. We could have all those things. We would be running a business rather than working a job."

So Marney wrote in answer to the first question: "We want to be managing three workshops rather than working one."

"Hey, nothing's decided yet," Jim cautioned, yet warming to the idea.

"Sure, but we can change that later if we want – but do you think that's what the question meant?" Marney asked, thinking further.

"What else could it mean?" Jim answered.

"Well, does it mean what we want to be doing in business, or what we want to be doing in our lives?" Marney continued, "I think it may be the latter."

"There is no difference," Jim said.

"No," said Marney, "not as things are now, but there could be."

"Let's think about it."

After some discussion they decided that in five years' time they wanted to be enjoying some of the things they had forgone in recent years. They wanted to have a life outside the business. But they agreed they needed the business to provide for that life.

They added the following to their answer to question one: "We want to be taking annual holidays overseas, and to have enough capital to upgrade our house."

They then went on to the next question.

Question 2: What do you want to be doing in ten years' time?

After a lot of discussion they answered: "We want to own another three workshops, but this time in NSW."

Question 3: What do you want your business to look like when you are finished with it?

"We want to have locations in Queensland, NSW and Victoria," they wrote.

Question 4: When do you want to be finished with your business?

"In 15 years' time," Jim and Marney wrote. Jim would be 50 years old by then and looking forward to an early retirement.

"That was interesting," Marney said. "That is the first time we have sat down and talked about where we are going. I think we've achieved something here, at last we now have some goals."

I saw them on Monday evening. It was normal to work back at the office, so it was no hardship to see them out of hours. It just meant my day had to be re-arranged. Things I would have done when I saw them I did earlier. They handed me the sheet with the answers duly completed.

"Who should have been the doctor?" I joked as I noticed the scrawl which was far more easily read than my own.

Smiling they waited, whilst I read their answers.

"The purpose of these questions was for me to get your ideas on where you want your business to be when you sell it," I explained. "This is what we need to plan towards. We need to set in place the mechanism to enable you to achieve the goals you have set out. This is what business planning is about. Over time your ideas may change, but that is normal. The plan is not a static thing, it should evolve as your goals change."

"You should be working towards getting your business to where you want it to be when you are finished with it. You need a vision for this, hence question four. Sadly, my experience is that many people in small business have no idea where they are going. Over the weekend you differentiated yourself from those people. Now let's get down to work."

KEY POINTS

You need to know where you are heading to be able to prepare the map to help you get there.

Ask yourself the questions:

? What do I want to be doing in five years' time?

? What do I want to be doing in ten years' time?

? What do I want my business to look like when I am finished with it?

? When do I want to be finished with my business?

WHERE YOU WANT TO BE

There are three things to consider when deciding where you want your business to be. These are:

- The vision
- The mission
- The objectives.

The Vision

This is how you see your business at the end of the planning period. (In Jim and Marney's case, this is a 15-year period.) Your vision should include the products you will be selling and the markets you will be serving, as well as the size of the business and its financial profile. It should be achievable, realistic and measurable.

The Mission

The mission statement is a summary of what your business is about. It is an expression of the purpose of the business, of your business philosophy as related to the products or services you sell and the level of customer satisfaction you wish to maintain. Unfortunately, these are often nothing more than motherhood statements, too general to be of use. The following benefits are claimed for mission statements:

➡ They focus the efforts of the business on the achievement of its goals

➡ They get commitment from your staff

➡ They are useful public relation tools

➡ They can be used to inspire confidence in your customers.

If you decide to prepare one, ensure you state:

➡ The business you are in and why

➡ What your business is attempting to achieve

➡ How you do it

➡ What is different about how you do it.

In *Benchmarking Australia*, MacNeil, Testi, Cupples and Rimmer claim "the mission statement draws together what the organisation does, for whom, and what is unique or distinctive about its way of operating." They add: "The mission statement should identify the operating values and a set of critical success indicators, both financial and non-financial, which will be used to define success."

An example of a mission statement, from the old David Syme School of Business (since changed) is:

> *"Our mission is to provide high-quality, relevant and applied education and research for the business profession.*

We seek to achieve this through a process of continuous improvement.

A focus on our student clients and their employers characterises our operation."

The Objectives

Clearly stated objectives are an essential part of the planning process. The work of Peter Drucker, the doyen of American management consultants, gave rise to the theory of management by objectives. Although some argue that this is now outdated, it is very relevant to small business. From my viewpoint your goals are the core component of your plan. In his handout *Preparing & Implementing a Business Plan*, from a seminar presented by The Institute of Chartered Accountants in Australia, Peter Haslock establishes four rules for goal-setting. He says the objectives must be:

1. Realistic and achievable

2. Clear and precise

3. Capable of being measured

4. Established over a reasonable time frame.

Your goals must be specific, that is they must be clear and measurable. You must have some way of knowing when they have been achieved. For that reason generalised goals should be avoided. They are normally stated in terms such as net profit before or after tax, annual return on owners' equity, or percentage of market share.

Your business goals should reflect your personal goals. If they are at odds with each other it is unlikely they will be achieved. Your personal goals should include the time you want to spend in the business in the future, your desired lifestyle, the money you need to live that lifestyle, and the financial security you require. Your personal plan needs to be developed at the same time as your business plan and used as a reinforcement for that plan.

Complete the following table to show how you would like your business to look when you are finished with it.

HOW MY BUSINESS WILL LOOK

	When Done	In 5 Yrs' Time	In 3 Yrs' Time	In 1 Yr's Time
Sales	....	....	....	....
Gross Profit	....	....	....	....
Net Profit	....	....	....	....

WHERE IS YOUR BUSINESS NOW?

CASE STUDY   COLLECT AND COMPARE THE FIGURES

"The next step in preparing a business plan is to understand your business. If you don't understand the way your business operates there is no way you can prepare a workable business plan."

"What do you mean by that?" questioned Marney. "We spend so much time in our business that there would be something wrong with us if we didn't know how it works!"

"Not necessarily," I replied.

"I have prepared these figures from your latest financial statements," I said, handing my clients a summary of their business performance for the previous 12 months (see overleaf). "What I want to do is to look at where your business is today. From that we will see what has to be done to get it to where you want it to be tomorrow."

JIM'S CAR CARE CENTRE
BUSINESS PERFORMANCE SUMMARY 1998

Profit and Loss Account:

Sales	831,602
Less Cost of Goods Sold	423,452
Gross Profit	408,150
Expenses	334,802
Net Profit	$73,348

Balance Sheet:

Cash	310
Inventory	29,640
Sundry Debtors	12,568
Other Current Assets	1,067
	43,585
Plant and Equipment	68,663
	112,248
Bank Overdraft	48,207
Creditors	43,365
Borrowings	18,816
	110,388
Owners' Equity	$1,860

I then explained to them what this condensed summary of their financial statements revealed to me.

"Your sales equate to a turnover of $15,992 per week. This has produced a gross profit of $7,849 per week. From this, expenses (excluding your salaries of $35,000 each) have been paid, leaving a net profit before owners' salaries of $1,410 per week."

"Your figures show that your business earns 49.08 cents gross profit per dollar of sales. This is revealed by your gross margin. The gross margin is calculated by dividing the gross profit by sales."

$$Gross\ Margin = \frac{Gross\ Profit}{Sales} \times 100$$

"Further, you earn 8.8 cents profit from every dollar of sales. This is found by calculating the net margin, which is the percentage of net profit to sales."

$$Net\ Margin = \frac{Net\ Profit}{Sales} \times 100$$

"This is misleading, though. You need to be paid before you can say that you are earning a profit. After deducting your wages of $70,000 from the profit you are left with $3,348. This equates to earnings of 0.4 cents for every dollar of sales. A less than satisfactory return."

"How often do you think you turn over your stock each year?" I asked.

"We don't know," said Jim. "We just order stock as we need it. Our suppliers' reps come every month and we place orders according to our requirements. If we run short we ring and place another order during the month."

"Your figures show that inventory is being turned over 14.03 times per year (once every 26 days)," I said. "I learnt this by dividing your sales by the average amount of stock held."

$$Stockturn = \frac{Sales}{(Opening\ Stock + Closing\ Stock)/2}$$

"You are only carrying six days of debt. This is because the majority of your sales are on a cash basis. That is a big positive for your business."

$$Day's\ Debtors\ Outstanding = \frac{Year\ End\ Debtors}{Account\ Sales} \times 365$$

"As you can see, there is nothing difficult about these calculations, but they reveal a lot to me about how your business is running."

"The figures show that after deducting your wages you are achieving a 180% return on the funds you have invested in the business, but this is misleading. At the moment you are running your business on borrowed money. This is because you have drawn the profits over the years to acquire your house. This is not necessarily a problem, however, because you own your home and can offer that as security if the business needs funds."

"I'd rather not," said Jim. "We set up the company to protect our private assets in case business turned sour and we don't want to expose our house to any business risk."

I listened, understanding, but wondering how they were going to fund any expansion if they weren't willing to risk their own capital. Why would a lender want to take a majority interest in a family business that was barely making more than a wage for its owners?

"Business carries with it an element of risk. You need to be rewarded for that. If you could earn equivalent funds by having your money invested in a less risky area you would question being in the business. At the moment the business is highly geared and susceptible to a downturn."

Jim understood where I was coming from. I had started to do a health analysis of his business. The figures alone, whilst informative, meant little until compared to what other similar businesses were achieving.

"Jim, yourself and Marney excluded, I understand you have five employees. Is that right?" I asked.

"Yes," he replied. "We have three tradesmen, an apprentice, and a spare parts clerk on our team."

"What hourly rate do you charge them out at?"

"$35," was the answer.

"How many hours a week do you and Marney work?"

"Too many," Marney said, then added, "We both work 60 hours a week."

That didn't surprise me. Small business often means long hours.

"How many weeks' holidays do you take each year?" was my next question.

"Four," Marney replied, "but I wish it was more."

"That means you each work 2,880 hours in a year," I said, entering the figures into my computer.

"One more question. How many jobs do you do a year?"

"I'm not really sure," Jim admitted.

"Well, let's work it out," I said. "What would the average invoice amount to per job?"

"About $800," was the answer.

"So you would do about 1,050 jobs a year," I said. The turnover of $831,602 divided by $800 equated to 1,039. I rounded it up to 1,050. "That means you would do about 20 jobs a week."

"Yes, that would probably be right," said Jim.

This concerned but did not surprise me. Despite being totally involved in their business, my clients could not answer these questions accurately.

"Let us see how your business compares to some others," I said, reaching over to the printer and removing a report I had just run off comparing the business with those of the FMRC Benchmarks Motor Mechanics. Whilst Jim and Marney's business was a specialist one, that category was close enough for my analysis.

The FMRC Benchmarking Team (previously operating as the Financial Management Research Centre) is a private organisation which was originally a part of the University of New England, in Armidale, northern NSW. It publishes a series of financial profiles of Australian small business which it calls FMRC Business Benchmarks. These are an invaluable aid when analysing a small business. The Benchmarks help us see how a particular business compares to those included in the summaries.

	Jim's Car Care Centre	FMRC Benchmarks
Total Income	$831,602	$529,749
Gross Profit	49.08%	53.10%
Overheads	39.67%	38.82%
Net Profit (before owners' salaries)	9.41%	14.28%
Net Profit Owner Workhour	$13.58	$22.38
Income per Person	$118,800	$107,770
Income per Job	$792	$336
Total Personnel	7	5.25
Jobs p.a. per Tradesperson	350	468
Day's Stock on Hand	26	22
Day's Debtors	6	17
Hourly Rate	$35	$48.43

The Benchmarks were extracted from Business Benchmarks Version 10 Motor Mechanics (1997) Group 4 Turnover $350,000 or more.

"Your business is a little different to the normal repair shop as evidenced by your income of $792 per total job compared to the Benchmarks' $336," I said. "So the figures have to be looked at with that in mind, but they give us a useful insight as to where you are at the moment."

"Your turnover is greater than the average for the firms included. We have no idea what the range was in the sample, but your figures include sales from your wholesaling activities."

"They show that your gross margin is considerably less than that in the survey. Similarly your net profit before owners' salaries is 5% less than the comparison. You achieved $39,124 profit per working owner compared to $47,611 for those motor mechanic businesses turning over $350,000 or more in 1997. I realise your figures are for the 1998 year but obviously we don't have access to 1998 results."

"Both of you worked for $13.58 per hour compared to $22.38 for the average in the survey. This is in part a reflection of your hourly charge-out rate of $35 per hour compared to the average of $48.43. These are things we can address in the business plan."

"There are some favourable comparisons. I have only given you a summary of the printout but the obvious standout figure there is your far better debtors collection than the average firm. This reflects the amount of non account cash sales in your business as well as the tight credit control that Marney maintains." (Note: the Benchmarks' debtors figure is based on credit sales only.)

"Yep, I wouldn't want to owe her money!" Jim quipped, having remained silent whilst I had explained the report to them. He had no idea as to how his business compared to others and I could see it concerned him.

"I think that we have covered enough for today," I said. "You need time to digest what we have just been through, but I have another questionnaire for you to complete before we meet again. It is important that you give it careful attention, as the answers will form an important part of the plan."

With that they made another appointment and left the office.

✳   ✳   ✳   ✳   ✳

KEY POINTS

☞ It is important to assess where your business is at the moment. If you don't know where you are now, how can you plan where you are going in the future?

☞ You need to find out how your business compares to the industry averages so that your goals can be set realistically.

☞ Your accountant should be able to supply you with benchmark figures for most industries. If your business sector is not included in the FMRC figures, there are other publications – such as those prepared by the IBIS group – that can be accessed (at a cost) which will provide you with the information you need. Your state government small business advisory service will be able to help if your accountant cannot.

WHAT YOUR BUSINESS DOES

It is necessary to identify and prioritise what the business does. The first step is to make a list of everything that is done in the day-to-day running of your business, then determine which of these things add value and which don't. For those that are either neutral or have a value cost, you must then consider why you are doing them and eliminate them if they are unnecessary.

There are some administrative tasks which are necessary, but do not add value. These include record-keeping and those things that need to be done for legal reasons, such as complying with the taxation laws. Consider whether it is possible to streamline these and minimise their cost to your business. For example, the introduction of a computer may free staff to do other things in the business.

There may be some things you are doing because they have always been done, but are a drain on your resources. Once identified, these can be eliminated from your business. An example may be the maintenance of a mail book. What real purpose does it achieve? Is it necessary? How often is it referred to? Can it be eliminated?

List the things done in your business in a table such as the one below. For each item, enter a 'Y' or 'N' for yes or no in the column headed 'Does it Add Value?' Then enter a 'Y' or 'N' in the column titled 'Is it Necessary?' Lastly, for those where the answer is yes for either question, place a 'Y' or 'N' in the column titled 'Can it be Done Better?'

ACTIVITY REVIEW

Activity	Does it Add Value?	Is it Necessary?	Can it be Done Better?
....	....	....	....
....	....	....	....
....	....	....	....
....	....	....	....
....	....	....	....

Stop doing those things that do not add value and are not necessary. Then for those activities you believe you can do better, ask the following questions:

? Why is it done?

? Who does it?

? When is it done?

? How is it done?

? Why is it done the way it is done by whom it is done?

The answers may lead to a better way of doing them.

UNDERSTANDING YOUR INDUSTRY

CASE STUDY KNOWING YOUR BUSINESS

"Come on Walrus. You can do better than that!" I shouted as Jim hit a soft return from my weak backhand into the net.

Marney giggled and pushed him to the side as he handed her the ball. "Match point!" I laughed as she tossed the ball into the air. She stumbled, put off by my unsporting gamesmanship, and the ball went way past the fault line. "Yeeees!" I exclaimed as my wife returned the second serve deep into Jim's side of the court and she broke into laughter as he dived, missing the ball and ending the game. "Game, set and match. Watch it next time," Marney said, grinning widely, as we headed to the gazebo for an ice cold drink. Jim and Marney were keen to get things moving, and I had agreed to see them on a Sunday. I didn't normally make an exception to my rule of not bringing clients to my home, but I understood that their working hours would make it difficult to see me at any other time, plus I didn't really want to work back too late at the office.

"It's time to get down to some work," I said, and we headed to the study.

Once we were seated, I asked the couple, "Have you brought the questionnaire?" Jim opened his briefcase and handed it to me rather sombrely.

"What's up?" I asked, noting his apparent lack of enthusiasm.

"I can see what you meant," he replied. "We didn't know the answers to some of the questions. It seems we don't know as much about our business as we thought."

"You are not alone in that," I answered. "Most small business people are so busy working their business that they don't have time to manage it. But you have started a process that will put an end to that, so let's have a look at your answers."

Question	Answer
When did you start in this business?	1993
What does the business do?	Supplies and fits steering and suspension products. Performs wheel alignments, and is starting to do brake work.
How does the business operate?	From a 3,500 square foot workshop located on the Pacific Highway at Springwood. Open from 8 a.m. to 5 p.m. Monday to Friday, and from 8 a.m. to 4 p.m. Saturday.
What products do you market?	Motor vehicle steering and suspension products. Shock absorbers, springs, steering components, brakes, sway bars.

Question	Answer
What is the percentage of sales from each of these products?	Not known.
How do you price those products?	We try to sell them at a 5% discount to our competitors.
Why did you choose these products?	The products are essential to the motor industry.
What geographic market are you in?	Brisbane Southside.
What is the demography of that market?	We don't know.
How many potential customers do you have?	We are unsure.
Is the market growing?	Yes.

"We need to find the answers to those questions you had difficulty with," I said. "The fact that you couldn't provide some of the answers indicates that there may be more scope for improving your business than you imagine. You can only manage what you know. It seems that we are going to have to implement some systems that will give you the information."

"Let us start with the percentage of sales from each of your products. Are you sure that you don't have any idea?" I questioned.

"I have a rough idea but I can't be sure," Jim answered.

"Part of the plan will be to install a computer system to provide these in the future, but for the moment let's take an educated guess," I suggested.

After some discussion and calculations we came up with the following:

Product	% of Sales
Shock Absorbers	35%
Springs	20%
Steering Components	5%
Brakes	1%
Sway Bars	3%
Labour	36%

"It is essential that we know where your sales are coming from and their contribution to the profit. At the moment you don't. We need to address that, and quickly," I said.

"I am also concerned with your pricing policy," was my next comment.

"We have to compete," Marney responded.

"There are other ways to compete instead of discounting," I said. "I noticed that your gross profit percentage was lower than those seen in the FMRC Benchmarks. Your profit before owners' salaries was also lower. Do you understand the effect that discounting can have on your bottom line?"

"It obviously reduces it," Marney answered.

"Let me show you by how much," I said, handing them an analysis I had done some time ago (presented opposite). "The table shows the increase in sales volume that you have to achieve to maintain the profit level prior to giving a discount. For example, if your present gross profit percentage is 50% and you give a 5% discount, you will need to increase your sales volume by 11.11% to maintain your profitability."

"Let's look at it another way. The second table [shown on page 32] shows the percentage your sales may reduce by if you increase your price by a certain percentage."

THE COST OF DISCOUNTING

Gross Margin

Discount	5%	10%	15%	20%	25%	30%	35%	40%	45%	50%
2.5%	100.00%	33.33%	20.00%	14.29%	11.11%	9.09%	7.69%	6.67%	5.88%	5.26%
5.0%		100.00%	50.00%	33.33%	25.00%	20.00%	16.67%	14.29%	12.50%	11.11%
7.5%		300.00%	100.00%	60.00%	42.86%	33.33%	27.27%	23.08%	20.00%	17.65%
10.0%			500.00%	100.00%	66.67%	50.00%	40.00%	33.33%	28.57%	25.00%
12.5%				166.67%	100.00%	71.43%	55.56%	45.45%	38.46%	33.33%
15.0%				300.00%	150.00%	100.00%	75.00%	60.00%	50.00%	42.86%
17.5%				700.00%	233.33%	140.00%	100.00%	77.78%	63.64%	53.85%
20.0%					400.00%	200.00%	133.33%	100.00%	80.00%	66.67%

INCREASING MARGINS

Gross Margin

Increase	5%	10%	15%	20%	25%	30%	35%	40%	45%	50%
2.5%	33.33%	20.00%	14.29%	11.11%	9.09%	7.69%	6.67%	5.88%	5.26%	4.76%
5.0%	50.00%	33.33%	25.00%	20.00%	16.67%	14.29%	12.50%	11.11%	10.00%	9.09%
7.5%	60.00%	42.86%	33.33%	27.27%	23.08%	20.00%	17.65%	15.79%	14.29%	13.04%
10.0%	66.67%	50.00%	40.00%	33.33%	28.57%	25.00%	22.22%	20.00%	18.18%	16.67%
12.5%	71.43%	55.56%	45.45%	38.46%	33.33%	29.41%	26.32%	23.81%	21.74%	20.00%
15.0%	75.00%	60.00%	50.00%	42.86%	37.50%	33.33%	30.00%	27.27%	25.00%	23.08%
17.5%	77.78%	63.64%	53.85%	46.67%	41.18%	36.84%	33.33%	30.43%	28.00%	25.93%
20.0%	80.00%	66.67%	57.14%	50.00%	44.44%	40.00%	36.36%	33.33%	30.77%	28.57%

"If you increase your prices by 5% and your present gross profit percentage is 50%, you can lose 9.09% in sales volume before your profit will be reduced."

"I think we need to look at our pricing policy," Jim said, stating the obvious.

"Have a look at this." I handed Jim and Marney an extract from the Australian Bureau of Statistics (ABS) publication which showed the demographics of the Springwood and Brisbane areas. "Is that information useful to you?"

	Springwood	Brisbane
Population:	6,571	1,333,940
Employed Persons	3,224	574,961
% Employed	49.06%	43.10%
Age in Years:		
0-14	23.72%	22.64%
15-64	69.43%	65.76%
65 and Over	6.84%	11.60%
Birthplace:		
Australia	71.06%	77.43%
Other	28.94%	22.57%
Occupational Groups:		
Managers, Professionals & Para-professionals	28.2%	29.4%
Tradepersons	13.8%	13.2%
Clerks, Sales & Personal Service Workers	36.5%	22.3%
Plant Operators & Labourers	15.2%	18.9%
Household Incomes:		
0-$30,000	25.18%	41.75%
$30,001 and More	54.42%	42.18%
Partial Information or Don't Know	20.42%	16.07
Own or Buying Home	78.21%	69.48%

"Yes, where did you get it?" asked Marney. "I didn't know that was available."

"From the local library," I answered. "There is a wealth of statistical information available if you know where to look."

"It tells you a lot about the demography of your market and the potential customers in it. Let's have a break," I said, then called to my wife to bring some refreshments.

* * * * *

KEY POINTS

☞ You should complete the questionnaire in this chapter to ensure that you understand your business.

☞ Understanding your business also requires an understanding of the industry you are in.

☞ Seek help if you have difficulty in answering the questions.

KNOWING YOUR BUSINESS, PART II

Completion of the following tables will help you gain an understanding of your business, which will in turn help you in your planning.

TURNOVER

Month	$
July	....
August	....
September	....
October	....
November	....
December	....
January	....
February	....
March	....
April	....
May	....
June	....
ANNUAL SALES	

By Product	$
Best Selling Product	....
Second Best Selling Product	....
Third Best Selling Product	....
Fourth Best Selling Product	....
Fifth Best Selling Product	....
Remainder of Products	....

CUSTOMERS

Number of Customers ....

Number of Customers Gained per Year ....

Number of Customers Lost per Year ....

Number of Transactions per Year ....

Sales From Biggest Customer ....

Sales From Top Five Customers ....

Sales From Top Ten Customers ....

Sales From Remaining Customers ....

EMPLOYEES

Total Number of Employees ....

Sales ....

Technical or Professional ....

Support ....

OTHER

Average Stock Held in $ ....

Average Debtors ....

Hours Open ....

Hours per Employee ....

Hours You Work ....

From these figures you should calculate the following statistics.

SALES	$
Sales per Customer	....
Sales per Average Transaction	....
Sales per Employee	....
Sales per Technical Employee	....
Sales per Sales Staff	....

Month	%
July	....
August	....
September	....
October	....
November	....
December	....
January	....
February	....
March	....
April	....
May	....
June	....
ANNUAL SALES	

SALES (Cont'd)	%
Sales From Biggest Customer	....
Sales From Top Five Customers	....
Sales From Top Ten Customers	....
Sales From Remaining Customers	....
Sales of Best Selling Product	....
Sales of Second Best Selling Product	....
Sales of Third Best Selling Product	....
Sales of Fourth Best Selling Product	....
Sales of Fifth Best Selling Product	....
Sales of Remainder of Products	....

OTHER

Number of Days' Sales in Stock	....
Number of Days' Sales in Debtors	....
Sales per Hour	....
Sales per Employee	....
Sales per Owner	....

The information provided by this exercise may surprise you. Your business may improve considerably by measuring these statistics. Without them you are running your business in the dark.

UNDERSTANDING YOUR BUSINESS SECTOR

It is essential that, as well as understanding your business, you have an understanding of the business sector in which you operate.

The first thing to do is to define that sector. Then you need to identify the key players in it. From there you need to characterise the operating features of the industry:

? Is it capital or labour intensive?

? Is the competition aggressive?

? How many suppliers are there? Are the suppliers in a dominant position?

? How are the products distributed?

? What is the current state of the industry?

? Where is it at – is it cyclical?

? What are the future prospects for the industry?

? What are the demographic trends?

Then you need to ask whether there are any global trends that will affect the industry.

WHERE DO YOU FIND THE INDUSTRY INFORMATION?

There are a number of sources from which information about the industry you work in can be obtained. These include:

▶ *Commercial information houses.* These normally charge for the information and include Dunn & Bradstreet, IBIS, FMRC Benchmarking.

▶ *Trade associations.* Manufacturers, trade and professional associations often gather information about the sector they represent, which they will often make available at no or little cost.

- *Government bodies.* The various state small business development centres have access to information covering a wide range of business sectors. The Australian Bureau of Statistics may charge for the information you require, but their publications are also available at the state libraries.

- *University centres.* Research facilities at the various universities can be a source of information, e.g. the Centre for Retail Studies at Monash University in Victoria.

- *Other sources.* A search of the Internet will reveal other sources of information which will assist you to gather information about your business sector. The public libraries often have a limited number of industry-specific publications available in their reference sections.

5

ASSESSING YOUR STRENGTHS, OPPORTUNITIES, WEAKNESSES AND THREATS

SWOT ANALYSIS

"Let's take a sheet of paper and draw two lines, one vertical and one horizontal, through the middle of the page," I said as I reached for my ruler. "Now let's write a title at the top of each of the resulting four sections." I did this and wrote 'Strengths', 'Opportunities', 'Weaknesses' and 'Threats' as the section headings.

"What we are going to do is to make a critical analysis of your business. We have to be totally brutal here because if we are not, the benefits of doing it will be lost." I smiled reassuringly as I noticed Jim look up at Marney, the concern showing on his face. "We are going to list what you see as the strong points of your business, the opportunities you see for your business, what you see as the weaknesses of your business, and the things you believe threaten your business. Then we need to think of ways we can emphasise the strengths, take advantage of the opportunities, remedy the weaknesses and overcome the threats."

I looked at their completed questionnaire and noted the answers to the questions listed there.

Question	Answer
1. What are the things you do well in your business?	—Provide an excellent service. —Deal in quality products. —Offer an excellent after-care service.
2. What are the things you don't do well in your business?	—Motivate staff. —Staff training.
3. What things are happening in the economy that will help your business?	—Increased concern about car safety. —An increased acceptance of specialty businesses.
4. What things are happening in the economy that may harm your business?	—The trend to concentrate on price. —Consumer reluctance to spend. —Concern about the effect of the Asian downturn on our economy. —An increase in home-based mechanics.

I entered their answers under the headings on the worksheet as follows:

➠ Question 1 answers under *Strengths*

➠ Question 2 answers under *Weaknesses*

➠ Question 3 answers under *Opportunities*

➠ Question 4 answers under *Threats*.

I was concerned that there were other areas which had not been addressed. So I asked some more questions.

"Let's look at your record-keeping," I said, being fully aware of the weaknesses of James and Marney's system, and added, "Do you think it is adequate?"

"We would have no problem from a tax audit," James replied. "We issue invoices for everything we sell, we keep our suppliers' invoices and use Mind Your Own Business as our computer system."

"That wasn't the question," I said. "Are you aware of your daily cash on hand, bank balance and sales?"

"Not daily," Marney admitted.

"Are you aware of your weekly debtors' balances, creditors outstanding and stock levels?" I continued.

"Not weekly," was the answer.

"Do you prepare monthly bank reconciliations, profit and loss statements, balance sheets, budget variance reports and aged debtor and creditor trial balances?" I asked.

"You know we don't," was the sheepish reply. "We prepare these things when we have the time. We don't see them as being as important as keeping the business running."

"Yes," I acknowledged, "but you should. You need to keep good accounting records for your own management purposes as well as for the tax man. If you don't, you can't plan and control your business. You are not alone in this. Many small business people look on record-keeping as a compliance requirement, rather than as providing the base data from which you can measure your performance. They fail to appreciate that they need to measure their performance to be able to improve it."

"I think we had better list that as a weakness," I added, noting the furrowing of Jim's forehead.

"There are other areas we should consider," I said. "The purpose of these questions is to provide us with information that will help us identify the things you need to do to achieve your objectives." We then discussed the matters set out in the remainder of this chapter.

* * * * *

KEY POINTS

☞ Identifying the strengths, weaknesses, opportunities of and threats facing your business is an essential part of business planning.

☞ It is important that all areas of the business are considered. To do less will result in an incomplete analysis.

☞ Don't rush through this exercise. It will help you uncover many things you may have not been aware of about your business.

☞ A SWOT analysis will enable you to critically assess where your business is and the likely emerging opportunities and threats. Once you become aware of them you can take corrective or remedial action.

SWOT ANALYSIS PART II

A SWOT analysis is a review of the strengths, weaknesses and opportunities of, and threats facing, a business. It is a vital exercise in highlighting the issues concerning a business and an essential element of any business plan.

To reiterate, the four elements in the SWOT analysis are:

▶ *Strengths.* The strengths of a business are the things it does well, the things that it does better than its competition.

▶ *Weaknesses.* Its weaknesses are the things it doesn't do as well as its competitors. These are the areas that need to be worked on so that the business can be improved.

▶ *Opportunities.* The opportunities of a business are the positive things that are occurring in the marketplace, things that a business can use to its advantage either now or in the future, the things that could be done that are not being done now.

▶ *Threats.* The threats are the elements that are potentially or actually damaging to the business. They are the issues that need to be addressed so they can be countered.

To cover these four areas requires both an internal and an external analysis. The internal analysis deals with the strengths and weaknesses. The external analysis deals with the opportunities and threats.

Completion of this analysis results in both an indication of the potential improvement in the business (stemming from the articulation of its strengths and opportunities) and the limits to its improvement (indicated by the weaknesses and threats).

The Internal Analysis

The internal analysis should disclose the core competencies of the business. These are the things that the business does better than its competitors. They give the business a sustainable competitive advantage that, when identified, can be:

⟹ controlled;

⟹ capitalised on;

⟹ protected; and

⟹ developed.

An example might be total control over the supply of a particular product. Coca Cola's core competency could be seen by some to be its brand image, BMW's could be seen to be its superior technology.

Yours could be that your business may have a unique location which provides you with an advantage. You can control such an advantage by making sure you have a lease. You can capitalise on it by promoting the location in your advertising. You can protect it by buying it. You can develop it by expanding the site.

The following areas should be analysed when considering the strengths and weaknesses of your business:

➠ The products you sell or the services you provide

➠ Your administration and reporting systems

➠ Your market position

➠ The technology and equipment you use

➠ Your financial position

➠ Your structure

➠ Your staff

➠ Your suppliers

➠ Your customers

➠ Your competition.

The External Analysis

The external analysis should reveal the positive and negative developments that are occurring in your marketplace. It should cover:

➠ The competition

➠ The political environment

➠ Government rules and regulations

➠ The state of the economy and its effect on your business

➠ New technology not being used by your business.

Completion of the table below will help you react to the positive and negative results of your findings.

	Implications	My Response
Opportunities		
1	....	....
2	....	....
3	....	....
4	....	....
5	....	....
Threats		
1	....	....
2	....	....
3	....	....
4	....	....
5	....	....

THE PRODUCTS OR SERVICES YOU SELL

List the features of the products or services you sell. What advantages and disadvantages do they have? Are they newly introduced into the market, are they mature or are they in danger of becoming obsolete? Are they appropriate to the customers you serve? Are there any products you stock that are slow-moving and which tie up your working capital? Do you stock an adequate range?

Where do your products fit in the marketplace? Are they:

➠ Low, medium or high quality?

➠ Low, medium or high priced?

➠ Low, medium or high volume?

Prepare a table as below, entering an 'L' for Low, 'M' for medium, and 'H' for high, and consider whether your answers are consistent with the market niche you are trying to fill. Look to see if there is any conflict in your product mix. Is there anything you are selling that doesn't fit? Is there a product or service you should be selling that you aren't?

Product	Quality	Price	Volume
....	....	....	....
....	....	....	....
....	....	....	....
....	....	....	....
....	....	....	....
....	....	....	....

Your products and services must meet your customers' needs. It is important that you provide products which fulfil the market's needs, not your own. Your tastes and preferences may be vastly different from those of your marketplace.

For each product you sell or each service you provide, rank them on a scale of 1 to 5, with 1 being poor and 5 being excellent. Use a table such as the one below (making it as big as you need) and use the results to decide whether you need to replace or add to the products you are providing.

Product	Presentation	Availability	Delivery	Performance	Quality	Appropriateness
....	....	....	....	....	....	....
....	....	....	....	....	....	....
....	....	....	....	....	....	....
....	....	....	....	....	....	....
....	....	....	....	....	....	....
....	....	....	....	....	....	....

The following questions may help in the ranking process:

▶ *Presentation.* How are your products packaged and presented? Are they attractive, stylish or otherwise? Do they need to be?

- *Availability.* Are you able to provide prompt service? Do you have sufficient numbers in stock? Can you get timely supply from your suppliers?

- *Delivery.* Can you provide prompt delivery?

- *Performance.* Do the products meet an appropriate performance standard?

- *Quality.* Are the products of a satisfactory quality?

- *Appropriateness.* Do the products and services fit in with the other products and services you provide?

YOUR REPORTING SYSTEMS

Good record-keeping is an essential part of the planning and control of your business. The reports which you use to manage your business are only as good as the records on which they are based. If you have inaccurate information you will make inaccurate decisions and prepare unrealistic budgets. For this reason you need to question whether your reporting system provides you with timely and accurate information which enables you to effectively manage your business and prepare and monitor your business plan.

Your system should:

➟ Enable the preparation of accurate financial reports

➟ Provide the substantiation for the figures in those reports

➟ Comply with the taxation and company laws on record-keeping

➟ Avoid duplication of entry of information

➟ Be appropriate to your needs

➟ Be timely.

Consider the following:

? Is entry to your computer system restricted by password?

? Are your source documents consecutively numbered?

? Are goods received checked against purchase orders and invoices?

? Do you perform periodic stocktakes and check the results against your inventory records?

? Are bank reconciliations prepared monthly?

? Do you prepare monthly financial reports?

? Does your system report your key performance indicators?

? Does your system provide you with details as to your turnover, your gross profit, your expenses, your net profit, your bank balance, your inventory, your debtors and your creditors?

? Are backups taken from your computer system?

? Are copies of your backups stored off-site?

YOUR MARKET POSITION

Where do you stand in the market? How big is your market share? Much has been written about the need to compare your market share against that of your competitors. But how do you do it? You know your turnover, but how can you know that of your competitors? It is easier for public companies because they can look at the published accounts for others in their industry and extract the figures from them. They can measure the total market from their own research, the research published by various economic research organisations or from information from industry organisations or the Australian Bureau of Statistics. But it is different for small businesses. Where do you get the information that is relevant to your own business, and at what cost? The reality is that most times you will not be able to, or not with complete accuracy anyway. But then, do you really need to be totally accurate or will a general idea suffice? I suspect it will – and there is a way, flawed though it may be, to get it.

Firstly, contact your industry organisation and ask whether market figures are available, and if so, where you can obtain them. If they are available, then use them. If they are not, then the following approach may be worth considering. This involves using the figures published by the FMRC Benchmarking Team. Where possible these are categorised in three ways:

1. Turnover

2. Net profit per working owner

3. Location.

The Benchmarks for Bakery & Hot Bread Shops (1997), for example, are broken up into the following location categories:

➠ Capital city, large regional city or suburbs

➠ Other cities/towns with population greater than 20,000

➠ Towns with population up to 20,000

➠ All businesses with rented premises

➠ Rented premises located in arcade or shopping centre.

These categories differ for various business types reported by the Benchmarking Team. For example, the 1997 Benchmarks for Fruit and Vegetable Retailers display location figures under the following category groups:

➠ Capital city, large regional city or suburbs

➠ Other cities/towns with population greater than 20,000

➠ Towns with population up to 20,000

➠ Businesses with rented premises

➠ Essentially owner operated.

Once you have categorised the geographic location in which your business operates, make a list of your competitors. Multiply the number of competitors by the income reported in the Benchmarks to obtain an estimate of the total turnover for the market you are serving (see the example overleaf).

Check this by comparing the staff numbers employed by your competitors, a figure that should not be difficult to obtain through observation, or by asking your suppliers. See how this compares to the Benchmark figure. If it is materially different from the Benchmarks, adjust the average turnover figures by dividing the turnover by the number of employees and multiply that out accordingly. This method can also be used to estimate the individual turnover of your competitors.

Overall, the method has flaws:

➧ It relies on the adequacy of the sampling performed by the FMRC Team. The number of businesses in the samples vary widely. In their version 10 Benchmarks there are 94 sectors covered. The number of businesses in each sector ranges from six (Health Food Retailers, Screen Printers, and Video Libraries) to 141 (Veterinary Practices).

➧ It assumes that the averages are indicative of your competitors, and your geographic area, which they may not be.

➧ It assumes that the productivity of your competitors is in line with those of the Benchmarks.

But it is a start.

EXAMPLE

Let us assume you operate a bookshop in a capital city. Your turnover is $600,000. There are three other bookshops in your geographic area. They employ staff as follows:

Competitor 1   4

Competitor 2   3

Competitor 3   5

The FMRC Benchmarks indicate that the average annual income for bookshops in capital cities is $678,419 and that the average number of full-time equivalent employees is 3.76. To get the estimated total market turnover we multiply the Benchmark turnover by three. (This is the total number of bookshops in your market area. The average number of employees for the stores approximates those of the Benchmark figures so there is no need to adjust for employee numbers.) This gives us $2,035,257, which we round off to $2,035,000. We then add our known turnover of $600,000 for your store to give us an estimated market turnover for your area of $2,635,000.

We now calculate an estimated turnover for your competitors:

Competitor 1 $678,300

Competitor 2 $508,700

Competitor 3 $848,000

These figures were obtained as follows:

Competitor 1 = $2,035,000 divided by 3 then rounded.

Competitor 2 =	$2,035,000 divided by 12 (the total number employed by your competitors) then multiplied by 3 (this competitor's employee numbers).
Competitor 3 =	the balance.

With this information we can now allocate market share in percentage terms:

	Turnover	**Market Share**
Your Firm	$600,000	23%
Competitor 1	$678,300	26%
Competitor 2	$508,700	19%
Competitor 3	$848,000	32%
TOTAL	$2,635,000	100%

THE TECHNOLOGY AND EQUIPMENT YOU USE

The use of up-to-date technology can assist in increasing production and decreasing costs. You need to consider whether your equipment meets your needs. However, you should not upgrade just for the sake of having the latest technology. There must be a benefit, whether it is in efficiency, cost or both, to warrant the expenditure. Computerisation and an increasingly widespread use of the Internet have resulted in an information explosion and new business opportunities. Mobile telephones have changed the way a lot of business is done, but have also resulted in an increase in the communication costs incurred by businesses.

You need to consider:

➠ The impact of any new technology on your business

➠ How new technology could improve your operations

➠ Whether your current technology and equipment are limiting your business performance.

With this in mind you should review the equipment used in your business, considering whether it should be replaced, and if not when it will need to be replaced. Prepare a list of your business equipment and complete the table below:

Equipment	Is it Suitable?	Date to Replace	Cost to Replace
....	....	....	....
....	....	....	....
....	....	....	....
....	....	....	....
....	....	....	....

The result will be an asset replacement schedule which will help you with your capital asset budgeting, and alert you to possible funding requirements.

YOUR FINANCIAL POSITION

A study by A.J. Williams of the survival and failure rates of new small firms in Australia for the years 1973 to 1985 found that 32.8% of small business failure is the result of financial mismanagement and cash problems. It is essential that you undertake a financial health analysis of your business to consider whether you are able to meet your current needs as well as whether they will enable the attainment of your future plans. This involves the calculation of some simple ratios. By comparing the ratios to those of prior years, trends will be revealed that may disclose unfavourable developments. You can then identify those areas where change is necessary and incorporate these into your business plan.

The ratios can be grouped into four categories:

1. Liquidity

2. Profitability

3. Efficiency

4. Financial structure.

The key ratios of each category are listed below.

Liquidity

The liquidity ratios disclose the ability of the business to meet its current commitments.

- *Current ratio*. This shows how many dollars are available to pay each dollar of current debt.

- *Liquid ratio*. This discloses how many dollars are available to pay immediate debt.

The higher these ratios, the better.

Profitability

The profitability ratios are a measure of business performance. These are expressed in percentage terms.

- *Gross profit margin*. This shows the percentage of every dollar of sales that is available to meet your overheads and provide for profit.

- *Net profit margin.* This is a reflection of the overall efficiency of management. It shows the percentage of net profit that is left from every dollar of your sales.

- *Return on assets.* This is a measure of how well you are utilising the assets of your business.

- *Return on equity.* This discloses the percentage return on the money you have invested in your business.

Efficiency

The efficiency ratios disclose management competence.

- *Asset turnover.* This measures the utilisation of your business assets.

- *Debtor days.* This reflects the average collection period of account receivables, and the efficiency of your credit management.

- *Stockturn.* This measures the efficiency of inventory management.

Financial Structure

- *Gearing ratio.* This is an indicator of business risk.

Ratio	Formula
Current Ratio	$\dfrac{\text{Current Assets}}{\text{Current Liabilities}}$
Liquid Ratio	$\dfrac{\text{Current Assets} - \text{Stock}}{\text{Current Liabilities} - \text{Bank Overdraft}}$
Gross Profit Margin	$\dfrac{\text{Gross Profit}}{\text{Sales}}$

Ratio	Formula
Net Profit Margin	$\dfrac{\text{Net Profit}}{\text{Sales}}$
Return on Assets	$\dfrac{\text{Net Profit}}{\text{Total Assets}}$
Return on Equity	$\dfrac{\text{Net Profit}}{\text{Equity}}$
Asset Turnover	$\dfrac{\text{Sales}}{\text{Total Assets}}$
Debtor Days	$\dfrac{\text{Credit Sales}}{\text{Debtors}}$
Stockturn	$\dfrac{\text{Cost of Goods Sold}}{\text{Average Stock}}$
Gearing	$\dfrac{\text{Total Liabilities}}{\text{Total Assets}}$

These ratios are an essential ingredient in deciding the strategies to incorporate into your business plan.

Draw up a table as shown overleaf, calculate the ratios for your business and enter them in the appropriate columns. Five years is ideal to see a clear trend. Then enter an arrow in the extreme right column to indicate whether the trend is up, down or sideways.

Ratio	1999	1998	1997	1996	1995	Trend
Current Ratio	....	....	....	....	....	....
Liquid Ratio	....	....	....	....	....	....
Gross Profit Margin	....	....	....	....	....	....
Net Profit Margin	....	....	....	....	....	....
Return on Assets	....	....	....	....	....	....
Return on Equity	....	....	....	....	....	....
Asset Turnover	....	....	....	....	....	....
Debtor Days	....	....	....	....	....	....
Stockturn	....	....	....	....	....	....
Gearing	....	....	....	....	....	....

Ideal ratios vary from business to business. For example, whilst a 2:1 current ratio has historically been regarded as sound, it may not be necessary in a cash business. You may need to refer to your accountant for help with the analysis.

Use the table below for assistance in interpreting the trend.

Ratio	Ratio Increasing	Ratio Decreasing
Current Ratio	Favourable	Unfavourable
Liquid Ratio	Favourable	Unfavourable
Gross Profit Margin	Favourable	Unfavourable
Net Profit Margin	Favourable	Unfavourable
Return on Assets	Favourable	Unfavourable

Ratio	Ratio Increasing	Ratio Decreasing
Return on Equity	Favourable	Unfavourable
Asset Turnover	Favourable	Unfavourable
Debtor Days	Unfavourable	Favourable
Stockturn	Favourable	Unfavourable
Gearing	Unfavourable	Favourable

YOUR STRUCTURE

Your organisational structure has two parts. The first is the legal structure of your business. Is it a sole trader, a partnership, a company or a trust? The second is a consideration of the jobs performed in the business and the people who perform them.

The Legal Structure

Some thought should be given to the appropriateness of your business structure. You may have commenced trading some time ago as a sole trader. With growth in your business and change in circumstances you may then be better suited to a partnership, company or trust.

Consider:

➠ Your business size

➠ Your business objectives

➠ The number of owners

➠ The relationship of the owners

➠ The income from the business

➠ Your family situation

➠   Your estate planning needs

➠   The income levels of family members

➠   The age of family members

➠   Your age

➠   The risk of the business

➠   Protection of your assets

➠   Your financial situation

➠   The cost of establishment

➠   The costs of maintenance

➠   The taxation benefits

➠   Legal liabilities of the business.

As part of your planning process you should seek advice from your accountant as to whether your trading structure is still suitable for you. If not, ask him to set out the advantages and disadvantages of a changed structure, the costs of establishment, the annual costs of administrating the structure, the tax savings based on expected incomes, and why he has come to his conclusion. The decision to change the structure should not be taken lightly.

The Jobs Performed in the Business

It is important that you and your staff are aware of how responsibility is delegated and how work assignments are handled in your business. The organisation should be structured to ensure the business runs efficiently.

Your organisational structure should:

➠   Define the lines of authority

➠   Specify the jobs and the roles of staff.

You should draw up an organisational chart so that this is clearly defined, for example:

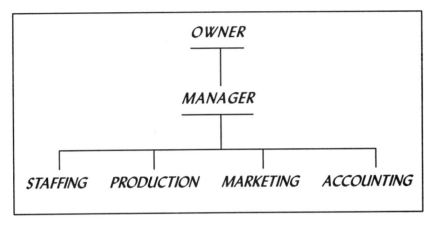

YOUR STAFF

The success of any business is dependent on the people in it. You should ensure your staff have the necessary skills needed for the business to function effectively. If your employees are weak in any areas you need to provide the appropriate training to overcome their deficiencies. To do this you need to consider the areas of knowledge and skill that are crucial to your business's success and how you intend to cope with any shortfall. This may require the hiring of new staff to provide for the need or the hiring of outside contractors.

The following areas should be addressed:

- Management skills
- Technical skills
- Marketing skills
- Operational skills.

Your employees must be motivated to help you to reach your goals. They should be committed and capable team members who want to make your business work. If they have contact with customers, they must be able to interact well with them. It is important that your recruitment policies are framed to find this type of person.

For each type of position, you should prepare a job analysis which formalises the job purpose, duties and level of responsibility. Find answers to the questions:

? How many employees do you need?

? Do your staff possess the skills necessary for their positions?

? Do you have a policy for the hiring and firing of your staff?

? What qualities do you look for in your employees?

? Are they aware of your expectations?

? Are they aware of your vision for the business?

? Do you have a training procedure in place?

? Do you provide them with performance standards?

? How do you measure whether they are meeting the standards?

? Do you discuss the results with them?

? How do you motivate them?

? Have your customer contact staff had training in:

➡ Selling?

➡ Telephone skills?

➡ Customer service?

YOUR SUPPLIERS

You must ensure that your suppliers are able to provide you with your products as and when you need them. You should question:

? Are your suppliers reliable?

? Do they supply products of acceptable quality?

? Are you tied to any particular supplier?

? Are you aware of all possible suppliers?

? Are the suppliers prepared to do business with you?

? Can the suppliers deliver on a timely basis?

? Can the suppliers meet your demand?

YOUR CUSTOMERS

Your customers are one of the most important elements of your business. Without them you do not have one! Satisfy their needs, treat them well and they will return and buy from you again. They may even refer other customers to you. Upset them and you may never see them again. Knowing who your customers are is a crucial element in devising a marketing plan. It you don't know the characteristics of your customers, how can you devise promotional strategies to target them? You need to understand your customers.

Customer Profile

Question	Answer
How many customers do you have?	....
Where are they located?	....
What do they buy?	....
How often do they buy?	....
How much do they spend?	....
When do they buy?	....

One way to learn about your customers and how they feel about your business is to ask them to complete a survey sheet after they have purchased from you. Perhaps you could offer some incentive. For example, a car service centre could offer a free check-up after 1,000 km of driving if customers return the completed form.

CUSTOMER SURVEY SHEET

Name: ....

Address: ....

Telephone: ....

What is your occupation? ....

How old are you? ....

How did you become aware of us? ....

How did you find our service?   1: Good

2: Fair

3: Indifferent

4: Poor

What influenced you in deciding to buy
from us rather than our competitors? ....

How could we have improved our
service to you? ....

Other comments ....

ASSESSING THE COMPETITION

Most businesses have competition in some form or another. Yours will be no exception. You need to identify who your competitors are and then break them up into two categories:

1. *Direct* competitors, who sell a similar product or service to you and sell to a similar market.

2. *Indirect* competitors, who either sell a different product or service to you but to a similar market, or sell the same service or product to a different market.

You will need to adopt different strategies to deal with each.

Identify how many competitors you have and consider whether they are a threat to your business. Then attempt to discover who they buy from. They may have a cheaper or better quality product or their suppliers may offer more favourable terms than those you are using. Next, find out who their customers are.

Identify your three strongest competitors, then analyse their strengths and weaknesses. Undertaking the competitive analysis which follows (see the worksheet on the next page) will help you identify the position of your business in the marketplace relative to your competitors, as well as helping you rank your competition and see how you compare. Give each of your three major competitors and your own business a score from 1 to 5 as follows:

1: Poor

2: Fair

3: Good

4: Very good

5: Excellent

Then total the scores.

Being aware of the strengths and weaknesses of your competitors will help you decide what to sell and how. You can learn a lot from them that will help you run your business successfully.

Note on paper:

➠ the main feature that sets you apart from your competitors

➠ the advantages you have over your competition

➠ the disadvantages you have compared to your competition.

COMPETITIVE ANALYSIS WORKSHEET

Ranking

Factor	Competitor 1	Competitor 2	Competitor 3	You
Product Range	....	....	....	....
Pricing	....	....	....	....
Quality of Product	....	....	....	....
Promotions	....	....	....	....
Customer Service	....	....	....	....
Staff	....	....	....	....
Location	....	....	....	....
Image in Marketplace	....	....	....	....
Size	....	....	....	....
Use of Technology	....	....	....	....
Distribution	....	....	....	....
Strategies	....	....	....	....
Market Share	....	....	....	....
Management	....	....	....	....
Length of Time Established	....	....	....	....
TOTAL SCORE				

How Should You React to the Competition?

Ask yourself what you can do to attract their customers to you. There is little point in trying to compete in areas where the competition is strong. It is better that you attempt to match these or differentiate yourself in some other way. You have little chance of competing with a discount chain on price. They have access to bulk-buying discounts that are not available to a smaller enterprise. You have to make up for this in some other way, for example by offering a better service or by adding value (see the next chapter).

The competitor analysis will enable you to rank their strengths and weaknesses. You should list them in the table below ranked from 1 to 5 (with 1 being the most significant strength or weakness). You should then note the implications of these to your business and how you intend to respond to them.

	Implications to My Business	My Response
Competitors' Strengths		
1	....	....
2	....	....
3	....	....
4	....	....
5	....	....
Competitors' Weaknesses		
1	....	....
2	....	....
3	....	....
4	....	....
5	....	....

6

ECONOMIC VALUE ADDED

 ASSESSING VALUE

"We have come a long way," I said as we sat back down in the study after a break for lunch. "It is time for me to show you something that I consider to be more important than anything else we have discussed today. You understand that you are in business for two reasons. The first is to provide you with a lifestyle and the second is to create wealth. What would you say if I told you that most people destroy rather than create value in their business?"

"That can't be," Jim answered. "I have many friends who have been in business for a long time and they are still there running along nicely."

"I didn't say they destroy their business," I replied, "I said they destroy value in their business."

"What do you mean?" Marney asked.

"Let me explain," I responded. "Traditionally, accountants have measured business success by performing analyses on financial statements such as the one we did when we looked at the strengths and weaknesses of your business. Sadly, the traditional methods don't always tell the full story. We need to look at things in a different way to see whether or not your business is creating value for you – and if it is not, then we need to address this in your business plan."

"There is a concept called *economic value added*," I continued. "This takes the view that unless the business provides a positive economic profit it will have lost rather than improved value. In 1991 an American management consultant called G. Bennett Stewart III published a method used by his company, Stern Stewart & Co., to review corporate performance. This methodology forms the basis of a computer program called Strategic Focus which I use in my practice. I have used this to do an analysis of your business. I think you might find the results enlightening."

I then handed Jim and Marney a summary, prepared using Strategic Focus, which is reproduced below.

Note	Performance Measurement	Actual	Target
1	Value Added	1,079	Positive
2	Economic Return on Capital Employed	13.27	Exceed Cost of Capital (11.5%)
3	Capital Turnover	13.63	2.00 to 2.10
4	Net Operating Profit After Tax	0.97	4.00 to 5.00
5	Return on Capital Employed (ROCE)	18.02	Exceed Net Interest (12.8%)
6	Activity	11.84	1.8 to 2.00
7	Profitability (%)	1.52	8.00 to 10.00%
8	Accounts Receivable Days	6	17 to 25

Note	Performance Measurement	Actual	Target
9	Product Inventory Days	26	18 to 26
10	Accounts Payable Days	36	30 to 40
11	Gross Profit (%)	49.08	47.97 to 53.10
12	Fixed Expenses (%)	46.40	20.37 to 38.82
13	Net Interest (%)	12.80	8.00 to 10.00
14	Debt-to-Equity Ratio	3,586.72	100.00
15	Working Capital (%)	0.19	20.00 to 25.00
16	Marginal Cash Flow	407,668	Positive
17	Net Cash Flow	-6,893	Refer Notes
18	Sustainable Growth Rate	55.00	Positive

1. Value Added

Value has been added to your business. This is because the economic return on capital employed exceeded the weighted average cost of capital (see page 84 for an explanation of the latter). This means that the net operating profit after tax (but before interest), NOPAT, was sufficient to cover the interest for the year and left a residual amount as a return for yourself which was greater than the return you could expect from an investment in an equally risky alternative. In your case this is the result of the high leverage employed by your business, which in turn is the result of your drawing of profits made to apply against your home loan.

2. Economic Return on Capital Employed

The economic return on capital employed reflects the amount of NOPAT as a percentage of total capital employed in the business.

This reveals the productivity of total capital employed and is a meaningful way by which the financial performance of a business can be measured. The economic return on capital employed should exceed the weighted average rate of capital. This was achieved in the year reviewed.

3. Capital Turnover

Capital turnover is calculated by dividing revenue by the total economic capital employed. The total economic capital employed is debt plus equity plus other funding, or (expressed in another way) working capital plus non-current assets. The ratio is an efficiency measurement. It measures the input necessary to calculate the NOPAT. As the investment in total net assets increases, the amount of capital employed increases and if sales remain constant, capital turnover will decline.

4. Net Operating Profit After Tax

NOPAT is calculated by subtracting all operating costs (excluding interest) and tax from turnover. The NOPAT percentage shows the relationship between NOPAT and revenue and measures operational performance. It is driven by price, volume, cost of sales and expenses. For the year your NOPAT percentage did not achieve the target. This indicates an unacceptable operating efficiency level and needs to be addressed.

5. Return on Capital Employed

Return on capital employed (ROCE) is calculated by dividing earnings before interest and tax (EBIT) by total capital employed. It links the operational performance in the profit and loss account with the operational performance in the balance sheet. It is the product of profitability and activity. If it is less than the average interest rate for the year, reverse leverage will occur, meaning the business will lose money on its borrowings. If this happens, equity will be eroded. In the year considered, your ROCE exceeded the net interest rate.

6. Activity

Activity measures the amount of turnover generated by each dollar of capital employed. It measures how efficiently the resources of the business have been managed. The main drivers of activity are debtors, stock on hand, creditors and non-current assets. The activity for the year exceeded the target.

7. Profitability

Profitability represents the operating performance of the business expressed as a return on sales after all costs except interest and tax have been covered. It is a measure of operational performance. It is driven by price, volume, cost of sales and expenses. In the year reviewed the targeted profitability was not achieved.

8. Accounts Receivable Days

The accounts receivable days represent the number of days of average credit sales that are unpaid at the end of the year. The target depends on the normal credit terms that are offered by the business. The accounts receivable days for the year were better than the target.

9. Product Inventory Days

The product inventory days represent the amount of stock on hand at the end of the year expressed as the number of days of average cost of sales. The target for this measurement is based on an assessment of the level of stock required to provide an adequate level of service to your customers. This was within target for the year analysed.

10. Accounts Payable Days

The accounts payable days represent the amount your business owes to trade creditors expressed as the number of days of average cost of sales. The acceptable level is dependent upon the credit terms allowed by your suppliers. At the end of the year under consideration the accounts payable days were within target.

11. Gross Profit

Gross profit percentage represents the percentage of sales available to cover your overheads and profit after the cost of sales has been covered. It reflects the average margin based on the sales product mix and is driven by price, volume and product mix. The gross profit for this period was within target.

12. Fixed Expenses

Fixed expenses are those expenses that do not vary directly with sales. The ratio represents the percentage of sales consumed by those expenses. It was higher for the year than expected and should be investigated.

13. Net Interest

The net interest percentage is the average interest rate paid on net loans. The target is dependent on the mix of the different types of finance used by the business. The ratio exceeded target in the year considered. The reasons for this need to be investigated.

14. Debt-to-Equity Ratio

The debt-to-equity ratio is calculated by dividing your total short-term and long-term debt by equity and is a measure of the manner in which you finance your business operations. The greater the ratio, the more reliance there is on debt and the less protection exists for lenders to rely on equity if your business runs into difficulty. Most businesses formulate their capital structure towards a target debt-to-equity ratio. This is usually designed to optimise the weighted average cost of capital. The more risky the NOPAT, the lower the debt-to-equity ratio because businesses find it difficult to borrow in these circumstances. Generally, lenders view a debt-to-equity ratio of 100% (i.e. a 1:1 ratio) as being the upper limit of what is acceptable. At the end of this year your debt-to-equity ratio was higher than the target. This was because your weighted average cost of capital was higher than the optimum. This is a result of the profits having been drawn from the business over the years to repay your home loan.

15. Working Capital

The working capital percentage measures the amount of sales which is invested in your working capital. It represents the incremental investment in working capital for each additional dollar of sales. Working capital is the excess of current assets over current liabilities. It is affected by your control of debtors and stock and the management of creditors. For the year analysed, your working capital percentage was lower than the target. This shows a high level of efficiency but may mean your business is heading for financial stress because stock is too low to service customers or creditors are being extended beyond sustainable levels. The reasons for this situation should be established and corrective action taken if necessary.

16. Marginal Cash Flow

The marginal cash flow represents the cash flow generated from each dollar of additional revenue less the cash outflows required to cover your incremental variable cost of sales, incremental variable expenses and the working capital percentage. For the year reviewed your marginal cash flow was positive.

17. Net Cash Flow

Net cash flow shows the change that took place in the net loan position of your business between the beginning and end of the year. Your net loans are made up of all forms of debt finance employed by your business less any temporary cash on hand. For this year your net cash flow was negative. This means your net loans have increased.

18. Sustainable Growth Rate

The sustainable growth rate is calculated by dividing the retained income for the year by the opening equity. It is the maximum amount by which a business can increase its turnover and investment in net assets without changing the way it operates and without changing its debt-to-equity ratio. It is a complex area and has many elements. These include interest, taxation, dividends and drawings, leverage, profitability and activity. All of these have an impact upon the ability of the business to grow. It is important to realise that if you plan for your business to grow at a greater rate than the sustainable growth rate, you will have to borrow a disproportionate amount in relation to the internally generated funds and your debt-to-equity ratio will deteriorate. In short, your business will become more risky. Viewed simplistically, a business can grow at a sustainable level if it can increase its turnover without increasing its expenses or employing more working capital. Because of this, it is important that sales budgets be prepared within your sustainable growth level. If they are not, then the way your business is operated must change. For the year the sustainable growth rate was in excess of the target.

"This analysis reveals a number of things we need to address in your business plan." I saw little point in explaining in any more detail the problems highlighted by the review. They were self-evident. At least to me they were, and Jim and Marney knew they were free to ask any questions they liked, and that I would explain it to them for as long as it took to ensure they understood. "My main concern is the high gearing you employ, which is the reason for the balance sheet efficiency ratios exceeding the targets. Things look better than they really are. You are running your business on other people's money and this carries with it a high degree of risk, particularly if you suffer a period of tight liquidity. I realise that you can offer your home as security if borrowings are required, but for a time profits are going to have to be left in the business so as to build up some equity."

"We need the money we are drawing at the moment to survive," Marney said, voicing her concern.

"I realise that," I said, adding, "But there are some strategies we can use to increase your profitability and by that, gain additional funds to enable yourselves to correct your equity situation. We will address those later."

✳ ✳ ✳ ✳ ✳

KEY POINT

☞ If your business does not earn an economic profit it will have lost value. The traditional accounting measures do not adequately reveal whether value has been created or destroyed. For this reason it is essential that you measure your economic value added and your economic rate of return on capital employed.

The sad reality is that most small businesses do not return their owners a positive profit. That is, their business reduces rather than increases their wealth. After considering the cost of the funds they have invested in and an arm's length compensation for the hours they put into the business, there is a reduction rather than an increase in net value. A concept has emerged in recent years called economic value added (EVA). This is seen as a critical measure of wealth creation. It is based on the premise that a positive economic profit must be returned for the owners.

It is measured by the formula:

$$EVA = (R - C^*) \times Capital\ Employed$$

Where:

R = economic rate of return

C^* = cost of capital

The average business fails the EVA test. Because the fundamental purpose of your business should be to increase your net worth, it must create value rather than destroy it. To do this it must provide an economic return. For this reason EVA is an important consideration in business planning. (Note: EVA is a trademark of Stern Stewart & Co.)

CALCULATING YOUR EVA

The Economic Rate of Return

The economic rate of return for a small business is calculated as follows:

1. Calculate your NOPAT (Net operating profit after tax)

(Net profit before tax + Interest paid + Owner's benefits – Arm's length owner's remuneration – Interest earned) x Your tax rate = NOPAT

The net profit before tax is obtained from your profit and loss statements.

Owners' benefits equals the total of all payments relating to yourself which have been included as an expense. This includes your wages, superannuation and any other expense on your behalf.

Arm's length owner's remuneration is what you would have had to pay an employee to perform the tasks you do in your business.

Your tax rate is the tax payable on your income divided by your taxable income. This is your average tax rate, not your marginal tax rate. Your marginal tax rate reflects the tax you pay on each additional dollar earned and is not a reflection of the percentage tax you pay on your income.

EXAMPLE

Net Profit Before Tax		40,000
Add:		
Owners' Salaries	40,000	
Owners' Superannuation	10,000	
Owners' Benefits	5,000	
Interest Paid	5,000	60,000
		100,000
Deduct:		
Arm's Length Remuneration		80,000
Net Operating Profit		20,000
Multiplied by:		
(1 − Tax Rate)		64%
NOPAT		$12,800

2. Remove the effect of debt from your capital

Take the net assets figure from your balance sheet. This is because assets – liabilities = net assets and net assets = equity. Taking the net asset figure will allow for different equity treatments by accountants when preparing special purpose accounts. Add to this shareholder loans, beneficiary loans and any other figure included under current or non-current liabilities which represents any money you have lent the business. Subtract any similar figure disclosed as an asset. This results in your adjusted equity. Add to this all interest bearing debt. The figures used should be the figures for the previous financial year. This is because we want to measure the return on your capital. The net assets for the current year will include the effect of both financing decisions and operating results for the current year.

EXAMPLE

Previous Financial Year:

Net Assets	70,000
Shareholder's Loans	20,000
Bank Loan	30,000
Adjusted Capital	$120,000

3. Divide NOPAT by the adjusted capital to get the economic rate of return

EXAMPLE

NOPAT	=	$12,800
Adjusted Capital	=	$120,000
Economic Rate of Return	=	10.7%

The Cost of Capital

Capital represents your equity. That is the amount of money you have invested in your business. If you operate as a sole trader or partnership this figure is equivalent to the amount described on your balance sheet as net assets. If your business is operated through a company you should add the total of shareholders' loans to the net asset figure if they are disclosed as a liability, or subtract it if they are disclosed as an asset. Similar treatment should be applied to beneficiary loans if you operate through a trust. The cost of capital is the minimum rate of return required to compensate your lenders and yourself for risk. In the EVA paradigm it is the cut-off rate that needs to be earned to create value.

Your cost of capital can be calculated as follows:

1. Determine the cost of borrowing

EXAMPLE

Tax Rate $\qquad$ = 36%

Cost of Borrowing Funds = Interest Rate x (1 − Tax Rate)

$\qquad$ = 8 x 0.64

$\qquad$ = 5.12%

2. Calculate the risk free rate of interest

Take the interest rate for 10-year government bonds. This figure is published each day in the *Australian Financial Review*. This is called the risk free rate. This is because it is perceived that there is no risk of losing any money you have invested in government securities.

3. Calculate the business risk

Add to this a premium which accounts for the additional return required to compensate you for risk taken by your business. A study by Ibbotson Associates (Chicago, 1990) of security prices from 1925 to 1989 revealed that share investors were compensated by a 6% premium for bearing the risk of shares in comparison to bonds. On this basis a rate of between 6% and 8% can be estimated as being a reasonable factor to apportion to business risk.

4. Calculate your risk index

This is commonly referred to as 'beta', the risk of your business in relation to the market as a whole. Beta factors for listed companies can be obtained from a stockbroker. These can be used in assessing your risk index. I suggest that you should add a factor of 0.25 of a percent to account for the additional risk attached to small business. What you are trying to achieve here is to scale the risk attached to your particular business to the overall risk of being in business. The risk index is multiplied by your business risk, then the result is added to the risk free rate of interest to provide your cost of equity. Whilst acknowledging that small business is very different to the businesses of those companies traded on the stock exchange, this is a practical approach which will result in a more accurate result than other more subjective methods.

EXAMPLE

Risk Free Rate	= 6%
Business Risk	= 8%
Risk Premium	= 1.5
Cost of Equity	= Risk Free Rate + (Business Risk x Risk Premium)
	= 6 + (8 x 1.5)
	= 18%

5. Calculate the ratio of your debt to capital

Now you need to calculate the ratio of your interest bearing debt to capital. This is used to determine the weighting of debt and the funds you have invested in your business to provide your cost of capital. Remember that you need to include in your capital figure shareholder loans, beneficiary loans and any other figure included under current or non-current liabilities which represents any money you have lent your business. We use the targeted debt to capital ratio for this purpose.

EXAMPLE

Your budgeted balance sheet shows:

Bank Loans	$40,000
Owner's Equity	$60,000
Capital	$100,000

$$\text{Debt to Capital} = \frac{\text{Interest Bearing Debt}}{\text{Capital}}$$

$$= 40\%$$

6. Apply the weighting to the calculation

The cost of capital is the weighted cost of your business, i.e. debt plus equity.

EXAMPLE

Cost of Borrowing Funds = 5.12%

Cost of Equity = 18%

	Cost		Weight		Weighted Cost
Debt	5.12%	x	$\frac{4}{10}$	=	2.05
Equity	18.%	x	$\frac{6}{10}$	=	10.80
Cost of Capital (C*)				=	12.85%

CALCULATION OF EVA

Using the figures from our examples EVA is calculated as follows:

Economic Rate of Return = 10.7%

Cost of Capital   = 12.85%

Capital Employed   = $120,000

EVA   = (Economic Rate of Return −
                          Cost of Capital) x Capital Employed

                  = (10.7% − 12.85%) x $120,000

                  = -$2,580

This is not an uncommon example. EVA is a negative $2,580. Value has been destroyed in this business to the extent of $2,580. This means that the net operating profit after tax was not sufficient to cover both interest and the return an owner could expect from an investment carrying a similar level of risk. For value to be created the economic rate of return must exceed the cost of capital. This highlights the need for further investigation.

The preparation and ongoing utilisation of a business plan can help you increase your net worth. If you accept that the reason for being in business is to create value, then EVA becomes an essential part of the process. Overleaf is an EVA worksheet to help you obtain and work through your own figures.

AN EVA WORKSHEET

	Your Figures
NOPAT	
Net Profit Before Tax	....
Add	
Interest Paid	....
Your Wages	....
Your Superannuation	....
Your Other Benefits	....
	───────
Deduct	
Interest Earned	....
Arm's Length Owners' Wage	....
	───────
Multiply by	
1 – Your Tax Rate	....
NOPAT (Net Profit After Tax)	───────
Adjusted Capital	
Net Assets	....
Owners' Loans	....
Interest Bearing Borrowings	....
Capital Employed	───────
Economic Rate of Return (R) (NOPAT/Adjusted Capital)	....

Cost of Borrowing

Your Tax Rate ....

Your Bank Lending Rate ....

Cost of Borrowing
(Bank Rate x [1 − Your Tax Rate]) ....

Cost of Equity

Risk Free Rate of Interest ....

Business Risk ....

Risk Index ....

Cost of Equity

Debt to Capital

Interest Bearing Debt ....

Your Equity ....

Debt to Capital
(Interest Bearing Debt/Capital) ....

Weighted Average Cost of Capital (C*)

(1) After Tax Cost	(2) Target%	(3) = 1 x 2 Weighted Cost	
Debt			....
Equity			....
Weighted Average Cost of Capital			

EVA
([R − C*] x Capital Employed)

IDENTIFYING YOUR KEY PERFORMANCE INDICATORS

CASE STUDY   KEY PERFORMANCE INDICATORS

"If there was any one thing that is critical to the success of your business, what would it be?"

Jim's eyes lit up as I asked this question.

"That's easy," he answered. "Ensuring that the customers' cars are ready when promised, and that the job is done correctly the first time."

"How often does that happen?" I asked.

"Most of the time," was the answer, Jim's facial features tightening with an obvious discomfort.

"So you are saying that sometimes the jobs aren't ready as promised and sometimes the cars have to be returned because the job wasn't done right the first time."

"Sometimes," was the terse answer.

"How many times?" I asked again.

"We can't tell you that," Marney said.

"You mean you don't measure that?" I countered.

"Yes, we don't measure it but it would happen a couple of times a week."

"What do you do about that?" I asked.

"We apologise to the customer for the inconvenience, chastise the tradesman and fix the problem," was the answer.

"Is the tradesman aware of the time you have promised to have the car ready?" I queried.

"No. We know how long the job should take and allocate it accordingly," Jim said. I could see I had touched a sore point but it had to be pursued.

"So the tradesman is allocated the job, and then devotes his time to it until it is completed?" I asked.

"Yes, that's right." The answer was short and to the point again.

"He never leaves the job to do something else?" I suggested.

"Sometimes."

"How often does that happen?" I asked.

"Maybe a couple of times a day," said Jim, still agitated by the questioning.

"What does he do those couple of times a day?" I asked.

"Sometimes we may run out of parts and rather than send out for them, the tradesman will go and pick them up. That way he gets them quicker. Sometimes a problem crops up and we need to ask the tradesman to attend to it."

"So you don't always have the parts in stock?" I asked.

"No, but it is not possible to stock all the parts we may need," Jim said.

"So you don't check if you have the parts in stock before you start the job, and you don't check if you have the parts in stock before you tell the customer when his car will be ready."

"No, we don't do that, but we phone him and tell him of the problem."

"Always?" I asked.

"No, not always. Sometimes the tradesman forgets."

"So you end up with an unhappy customer," I said.

"Sometimes, but we do 60 jobs a week."

"So 3% of your jobs are either faulty or not completed on time," I said, noting Jim's discomfort.

"I guess so. I hadn't thought about it that way. But what can we do?"

"Well – when the customer books his car in, check that you have the necessary parts in stock. The work you do is specialised and involves modifying cars rather than repairing them. Sure, some of the work is repair but even then it is specialised, so there really isn't any excuse not to have the parts on hand. If you don't have the parts, order them in to make sure they arrive on time. If they don't arrive, contact the customer and explain the problem to him, and reschedule the work. Most people will understand. Even if they don't, that is better than taking the work in and not completing it on time."

"When the customer arrives," I continued, "write the expected time for completion of the job on the worksheet. Prepare another sheet which records the job number, the tradesman assigned to the job and the promised time for completion. Also record the actual time of completion. Make sure this form is completed and signed by the tradesman. This way he is aware that you are keeping a record and his signing of the form makes sure he takes responsibility for meeting the requirement. Keep a record of the number of jobs done and the number of jobs completed on time. Every Monday before work commences, relay the results to the tradesmen. Post the results on the firm's notice board. The tradesmen will begin to compete with each other to make sure they complete the jobs on time. If they don't, you would have to question their suitability as employees."

"Lay down a rule, that once assigned to a job, that job is to be given precedence over any other tasks that may arise. You have three others, including Marney and yourself, available to attend to any other problems that might occur."

"Keep a record of the number of jobs returned with problems. Note the problems. Again, discuss the return with the tradesmen. Ask why they happened and stress the need for quality control. Draw up a checklist of things that must be done, including a road test, before the vehicle is handed over to the customer. Have the person doing the tasks sign off on each of them. Ensure that the list is checked by someone else before the job is deemed to be complete."

"This won't really take that much time. But the effect will be significant. You defined an area that you must get right for your business to be successful, yet you have not been monitoring it. There are many non-financial areas of your business which should be reported on. If you don't monitor the performance of these you will be running your business like someone who watches the scoreboard rather than the ball when playing a game."

✳   ✳   ✳   ✳   ✳

KEY POINTS

☛ You need to identify those things that are critical to the success of your business.

☛ You then need to find a means of measuring them so that they can be managed.

In his seminar notes, *Preparing & Implementing a Business Plan*, Peter Haslock of Canterbury Consulting defines a strategy as "a broad statement as to how you are going to achieve a given objective." That objective could be referred to as a *strategic* objective. A critical success factor is something a business needs to get right to accomplish its strategic objective. It is any area in the business where poor performance will result in a reduction of the overall performance of the business. On the other hand, when operating smoothly, it helps in the success of a business. A key performance indicator is a means of measuring whether the business is achieving its critical success factors – in other words, how it is performing. The measure may be in units of time, volume, money or percentages.

An example may be a retail store identifying a critical success factor as getting people to buy once they have entered the shop. A key performance indicator could be the number of sales made per persons entering the store. This might be measured by installing a door counter (which records every entry and exit), and dividing the resulting data by two to get the number of people coming into the store. The conversion rate could then be calculated by dividing the result by the number of sales dockets issued, for the period surveyed.

It is essential that you are able to identify those areas in your business that you must get right to be successful. One way of doing this is to ask your customers what you have to do for them to continue to deal with you. You could do this by surveying the customers as to what they like, as well as what problems they experience when they do business with you. That is, by asking them what you are doing right as well as what you are doing wrong.

You must be aware of any frustrations your customers experience in doing business with you. By doing this you will end up with a list of critical success factors. There probably will be fewer than four or five of these. The key is in articulating them. Once they are found you must be able to monitor your success in maintaining them. This means you must be able to identify your key performance indicators. If you are unable to measure them you can not manage them.

Without knowing the reasons your customers choose to deal with your business rather than your competitors, it is not possible to design strategies to get them to:

➤ Buy from you;

➤ Buy more from you;

➤ Buy more often from you; and

➤ Refer other customers to you.

Understanding what your customers want or how they will benefit from use of your products or services will help you provide them with a service they can relate to. You can only learn this by asking them.

The steps:

◆ Determine the strategic objective

◆ Determine the critical success factor

◆ Determine the key performance indicator

◆ Monitor the key performance indicator

◆ Observe the business performance and relate it to the information being provided by the indicator.

It may help if you identify the management areas of your business and their aims. These might be described as follows:

Management Area	Aims
Marketing	Maximise profitable sales
Purchasing	Obtain the best terms and supply

Management Area	Aims
Production	Maximise output and efficiency
Staff	Maximise productivity
Administration	Manage effectively
Finance	Ensure the availability of adequate funding and maximise profits

Consider what the critical success factors are for each of these areas, and then the key performance indicators. Ensure that these are reported to you weekly.

Key performance indicators are tools you should use to help you manage your business. They can be both a measure of performance and a pointer to existing or emerging problems.

It is not possible to give a generic list of these. This is because they are dependent on the strategies and the things you must do to implement them. In their *Business Process Design and Performance Measurement* manual Results Accountants' Systems say: "To start with KPIs is like starting with a scoring system and then designing a game around it."

CUSTOMER FOCUS GROUPS

One way of learning the things you must get right for your business to succeed is to invite a group of your customers to your premises to discuss the things they like about the way you do business and the problems they experience when doing business with you. This can be a valuable exercise. Who better than your customers to tell you what you are doing right in your business as well as what you are doing wrong? Listen to them, because without them you have no business.

8

GROWING YOUR BUSINESS

IMPROVING PROFITS

"How many customers do you have?" I asked, knowing the answer from the work we did when reviewing the strengths and weaknesses of the business.

"525," was the answer.

I entered that figure into my computer. I was running a program called Targeting Business Results which is the creation of Results Accountants' Systems Pty Ltd.

"How many new customers do you gain each year?"

"I am guessing, but about 50," Jim said.

"That is 9.5% of your customers," I said. "Let's round it up to 10% and call it 53. After all, you are not really sure, are you?"

"No," Jim answered. "As I said, I am guessing."

So I entered 53 into the computer.

"What percentage of these customers do you lose each year?"

"About the same," said Jim, "There really hasn't been any growth in customer numbers."

"That is something we will have to address," I said, as I entered 53 into the computer again.

"What do you think the effect on your profits might be if we could gain a further 2% of customers per year and lose 2% fewer?" I questioned.

"You tell me," Jim said. "I haven't ever thought about it."

"Would you be surprised if I said that your profits would increase by $16,326?" I said, turning the screen of my computer so that Jim and Marney could see the effect of the strategy.

"That much?" Marney exclaimed in amazement. "Is that possible?"

"You can see as well as I can," I answered. "There are some strategies we can use to attract more customers, one of them is keeping a tight reign on the key performance indicator we discussed earlier. If you do that you may be amazed at the growth you achieve and the reduction in your customer attrition rate."

"Let's put those in our budgeted column."

	%	Now	%	Budgeted
Customer Base				
No. of Customers at Start of Yr		525		525
Add Customers Gained Each Yr	10	53	12	63
		578		588
Deduct Customers Lost Each Yr	10	53	8	42
CUSTOMER BASE		525		546

"How many times do your customers buy from you each year?" I asked.

"That varies," Jim said. "Some of the modification work is one-off and we won't see the customer until he replaces his car. Other sales are more frequent. We have two types of customers, the public and car yards. The car yards may bring vehicles in for modification once a month. The public may return to buy some of the parts we stock. On average, I would say maybe three times a year."

I realised that there was some work to be done in installing some reporting systems for Jim and Marney. Too many of their answers had been guesswork. They realised that also and had already commented on the need for change.

"Let's enter that into the computer," I said.

"Would it be unrealistic to say that we could maybe get the public to buy three times a year instead of two?" I asked next. (The effect of this on sales is shown in the table below.)

	%	Now	%	Budgeted
Sales Frequency				
No. of Times Customers Buy From You per Yr		2		3
No. of Sales per Customer per Yr		1,050		1,638

"I don't know how," Jim answered, "but I guess not. I suppose you have some suggestions to help with that as well."

"Not in the $2,000 fee," I joked. "Yes, I have some ideas, we will come to those later but for the moment let's look at the effect this will have on profits.", and I temporarily adjusted the customer acquisition and attrition rates back to their original states.

"You can see that, together with the changes made to the defection and growth rates, this increase in customer buying will result in a profit improvement of $204,075," I said. "You will probably need another two tradesmen to handle the increased work so let's increase your overheads by $80,000. That will still leave an increase of $124,075."

"Now let's look at that effect combined with the increase in your customer base," I added, showing them that an additional profit of $148,564 would be generated by the changes.

"The FMRC figures we reviewed earlier on disclosed that your gross margins were 49.08% compared to 53.10% in the firms making up the Benchmarks." This was something that had to be said and an obvious area for potential profit performance. "You are now aware of the costs of discounting, and your hourly rate of $35 for tradesmen compared unfavourably to the Benchmark figure of $48.43. It would seem to me that you have to start selling on service and not on price. Let's see how much additional profit would be provided just by increasing your margins to 52%."

"We couldn't do that," Marney said. "No one would buy from us, and look at the profit improvement that we can achieve from the changes you have already suggested to us."

"It is only your perception that no one will buy from you. Look at the tables I showed you earlier [see pages 31 and 32]. You can see how much business you can afford to lose before you start going backwards. But I don't think you will experience that. We are not talking about a large increase. I am not saying you should price yourself out of the market. Rather, I am saying you should price with the market. Increasing your gross profit margin to 52% would result in a profit increase of $24,283. Increasing your margin to 52% along with the other changes considered would result in additional profit of $186,445. Your profit before you pay yourselves would be $259,794. Does that excite you?" I asked.

"The changes don't appear to be that big, but the effect on profit is phenomenal!" Jim exclaimed, an incredulous smile broadening his face. "Why haven't you shown us this before?"

"Too much of our time is spent on compliance matters," I said. "Most accountants would prefer to do this sort of work rather than slaving over financial statement preparation and tax returns, but those are the bread and butter of our practices and many of us just don't have the time to make these suggestions to our clients. Moreover, many of the clients aren't interested. They don't realise how much they can be helped. They don't ask and we don't offer. We should, but we don't. Many clients would not be prepared to pay for this sort of work, yet from where I sit this is a far more valuable use of their accounting dollars. I suppose I should be letting clients such as yourselves know that this sort of help is available."

✳   ✳   ✳   ✳   ✳

KEY POINTS

☛ A number of small changes can lead to a dramatic improvement in profitability.

☛ The worksheet at the end of this chapter can be set up in a spreadsheet and the effect of changes to your profit seen by reference to the budgeted improvement at the bottom of the worksheet.

PLANNING TO INCREASE YOUR PROFITS

Increasing your turnover will not necessarily result in an increase in profitability. Your planning exercise should be undertaken with this in mind. The solution to increased profitability is not necessarily about growing your business, and you may not want to get any bigger than you are anyway. I can relate to that. In some instances less turnover with fewer customers with better margins can result in improved results. That may be your long-term goal. You may have no desire to have more employees, bring in partners, rent larger premises, or add branches. Some business owners are content with keeping their businesses the size they are and merely ensuring they earn a comfortable living. Others want to grow. For some reason, the management gurus have concluded that growth is the indicator of success. They have done small business a disservice by propagating that myth. Success is simply the attainment of your goals, and the growth of your business is not necessarily an indicator of success. It all comes back to the questions we asked at the start of this book:

What do I want to be doing with myself when I am finished with my business?

and

How can my business help me achieve that?

Success is getting there – to wherever your answers indicate – and business planning is about taking the steps to help you get there.

This having been said, you may be able to improve your bottom line by:

➠ Increasing the number of customers

➠ Increasing the amount the customer spends with you

➠ Increasing the number of times the customer buys from you.

However, this is only if you pay attention to the four profit drivers of:

1. Price

2. Volume

3. Variable costs

4. Fixed costs.

What effect does an increase or decrease of one of these factors have on your profit if each of the other three factors remain constant?

Profit Driver	Increase	Decrease
Price	Profits increase	Profits decrease
Volume	Profits increase	Profits decrease
Variable costs	Profits decrease	Profits increase
Fixed costs	Profits decrease	Profits increase

However, it is rare that a change will occur in any one of the drivers without affecting one of the others. This means that none of the factors can be considered in isolation. For example, if you increase your prices your sales volume may fall. But if the fall is more than compensated for by the rise in price then profitability will increase. The replacement of products with those of a higher quality may result in an increase in variable costs. Yet this may be more than compensated by a resultant increase in volume.

It is sufficient for you to know that any measures you put in place to improve your profit must either:

➠ Increase price

➠ Reduce costs or

➠ Increase productivity.

An increase in price or decrease in the cost of goods sold will result in an increase in gross profit. An increase in volume or reduction in fixed costs will increase productivity. The improvements do not need to be large to have a significant effect on your bottom line. To illustrate this, consider the sensitivity analysis below. It shows the result of a 5% change in the key variables. I first learned of this technique when reading *Small Business Financial Management in Australia*, by John W. English. He uses this tool to compare the effect of changes in key input areas on the return of owner's equity. Five key areas are analysed:

- Sales price

- Sales volume

- Cost of sales

- Operating expenses

- Total assets.

From the results we are able to see which of the variables is most effective in maximising the return on owners' equity.

	% Change	Net Profit	Net Profit Margin	Asset Turn-over	Return on Assets	Return on Equity	Change in ROE
Price	5	114,928	13.16	7.78	102.39	*	*
Volume	5	93,755	10.73	7.78	83.52	*	*
Cost of Sales	-5	94,520	11.37	7.41	84.21	*	*
Expenses	-5	90,088	10.83	7.41	80.26	*	*
Assets	-5	73,348	8.82	7.80	68.78	*	*
Current		73,348	8.82	7.41	65.34	*	*

ROE = Return on Owner's Equity
* = Figures too small to calculate on the equity base of $1,860 (from p. 18)

In this case it is clear that an increase in sales price and volume and a decrease in the cost of goods sold are the most effective means of improving the owners' return.

But is this where your emphasis should be? If you accept the economic value added paradigm, the answer is no. Our concentration should be on those things that add value. What effect would a 5% increase in the drivers have on EVA? This is answered in the table below.

	% Change	Profita- bility %	NOPAT %	EVA
Price	5	6.21	3.97	27,690
Volume	5	3.79	2.42	14,140
Cost of Sales	-5	4.07	2.60	14,639
Expenses	-5	3.90	2.50	13,735
Assets	-5			1,078
Current		1.52	0.97	1,078

EVA = Economic Value Added

The answer is the same as before – increasing sales price and volume, and decreasing the cost of goods sold is the best way to improve returns – but it is clear that, in this example, an increase in price has the greatest effect on economic value added and the emphasis is now on the percentage changes required to increase your economic profit.

INCREASING THE NUMBER OF CUSTOMERS

It is essential that you know how much you can afford to spend to acquire a new customer. This requires an understanding of a concept called the 'lifetime value' of a customer. If you have a customer who buys from you four times per year and spends $100 each time and remains a customer for five years, his lifetime value to your business is $2,000. Knowing this enables you to objectively analyse the cost effectiveness of your promotional expenditure. If your gross margin is 40% and it costs you $800 to obtain that customer you obviously need to rethink your promotional strategies, and quickly.

WHERE DO YOUR CUSTOMERS COME FROM?

Do you know where your new customers come from? Do you measure which of your promotional strategies generate the most enquiries? Do you know what percentage of these turn into sales? It is essential that you know where your customers come from. This knowledge will show you where you need to concentrate your promotional activities, or may point to a need to change the emphasis of your advertising. Completion of the table below may help.

YOUR CUSTOMERS COME FROM:

Source	Number	Sales ($)
Customer Referral	....	....
Other Business Referral	....	....
Trade Organisations	....	....
Advertising	....	....
Yellow Pages	....	....
Promotions	....	....

Some of the ways you can increase the number of customers who have dealings with you are discussed below.

Referrals

The easiest way to obtain new customers is by referral, by getting your satisfied customers to do your selling for you. The recommendations of friends and associates is a powerful tool that should be maximised to your advantage. Systems should be put in place so as to encourage your customers to tell their friends about you – and once in place, the effectiveness of these systems should be monitored.

The first and most obvious way to get referrals is to ask for them. Why not print a paragraph on the bottom of your invoices, something to the effect of: "*We value your business and would appreciate you telling your friends about us.*" Or: "*We thank you for your custom and look forward to serving you, your friends and associates in the future.*"

A takeaway shop near where I live has a sign on their wall which reads: "*If you like our food tell your friends about it; if you don't, then tell us.*"

My dentist has a sign which reads: "*Our practice continues to grow by referrals from our patients. Thank you for recommending us.*"

Another way of gaining new sales is to give your customers a gift voucher to pass on to their friends. That voucher may, for example, offer a free pen set or coffee mug when the holder of the voucher buys from you.

You and your staff should go out of your way to make it easy to deal with you. This may require you to review how your customers are greeted, how quickly they are attended to, how sympathetically their problems are resolved, the interest you and your sales staff show towards attending to their needs, the quality of your products and services, and the accessibility of your premises.

Host-Beneficiary Relationships

There is a powerful marketing concept that works on leverage, leverage of the customers of other businesses. It is known as a 'host-beneficiary' relationship and can be an effective tool to attract new customers to your business. It involves a joint venture with a non-competing business which has a similar type of customer to yours. You tap into their customer base by mailing them with offers for your products, and they tap into yours in the same way. Such marketing may involve offering to split the profits with the host. It is effective because the hard work has already been done – the prospects have been identified and the trust of the customers has been established. Jay Abraham, an American marketing guru, promoted this method on a seminar visit to Australia in the early 1990s, and his message is carried on by the people from Results Accountants' Systems. He is said to have advised:

> *Be generous with the host company when setting up the deal. If you can't get the host company to pay for the mailing, offer to pay for it yourself. Or offer them 60% instead of 50%. Or offer them 100% until they double their money, and a lower percentage thereafter. Offer them whatever it takes to do the joint venture with you. What do you care how much they make, since you're investing so little up front and have so much to gain yourself?*

(From *The Accountants' Boot Camp Session Notes*, 4-7 June 1992.)

Direct Mailings

It is important that you identify your potential customers and direct your promotional mailings to that market. Mailing lists can be purchased or host-beneficiary relationships can be established with other businesses to ensure your direct mailing campaign is not wasted.

Money Back Guarantees

Do not underestimate the advantage that can be attained by offering a 'no questions asked money back guarantee'. This takes the uncertainty out of buying from you. It transfers the risk from your customer to you and removes the element of fear that the product may not work or may not fulfil your customer's need. This makes it easier for a customer to make a decision to buy from you, particularly if no conditions are placed on the guarantee. The reality is that you most likely would give someone their money back if they came in and demanded it. So why not use it as a marketing tool to attract new customers and promote what you probably do anyway? The probabilities are that you will generate far more business than you lose through any dishonest customers taking advantage of it.

REVIEW THE EFFECTIVENESS OF YOUR ADVERTISING

How effective is your advertising? You can't know if you don't measure the response to various advertising strategies you may use. The key is to test and measure. Then when you find something that works, stay with it until it doesn't work anymore. Advertising is not cheap so don't be afraid to seek help. There are many competent advertising consultants who will assist you for a fee. Make sure you ask them for proof that their strategies have worked before engaging them.

HOLD DEMONSTRATIONS AND SPECIAL EVENTS

You can attract new customers to your business by promoting demonstrations of the products you sell. You can hold in-store events such as inviting customers to exclusive buying nights where they can take advantage of specials available only to people who have purchased from you before, and allowing them to bring a guest who can take advantage of the same offer. These guests will most likely become new customers.

INCREASE THE AMOUNT THE CUSTOMER SPENDS WITH YOU

On-Selling

Asking your customers if there is anything else they may need or making suggestions as to other items that will complement their purchase can increase your turnover significantly. For example, if you sell a pair of trousers you could suggest the customer might like to buy a belt. If you sell a shirt, you might suggest a tie that matches. If you sell a tennis racket you might ask your customer if he needs to buy any balls. Take care to ensure that you do this in a helpful and friendly way. You don't want to come across as being pushy. The method is an effective means of increasing the average transaction value.

Review Your Selling Ability

It may be that you need help with your selling techniques. It might be useful to attend seminars on selling and to read various selling books. Perhaps you should engage the help of a management consultant. Once you have discovered a selling technique that works, you should standardise it. Staff should be schooled so that the basic method is used throughout your business.

Provide Your Customers With Information

By discussing the products you sell, you may well alert the customer to a need he has not identified before. For example, a pet shop may have a customer who is considering buying some tropical fish. By alerting the customer to the need for frequent water changes and the dangers of chlorine and other impurities in our water supply, he will realise the need to purchase some water conditioner as well as the other things he needs to keep his pets healthy.

Sell Better Quality Products

Better quality products usually cost more. That may not always be the case but often is. Usually they carry higher profit margins as well. Other considerations aside, selling these products is an obvious way of increasing the dollar amount per unit sold.

Review the Way You Display Your Product

Poor product display will have an adverse effect on your sales. Reviewing and optimising your stock layouts may have a significant effect on turnover. It may be wise to seek help in this regard. This may be available at no cost from your suppliers, who will be keen to see that their products obtain maximum exposure. I am always bewildered at how some bookshops expect to sell stock when a large majority of their titles are displayed by their spine only.

Review the Range of Products You are Stocking

By offering your customers a wider range of products, products that complement the others you sell, you give your customers the opportunity to buy from you rather than your competitors.

INCREASE THE NUMBER OF TIMES THE CUSTOMER BUYS FROM YOU

The least expensive way to increase your turnover may be to increase the frequency of transactions. You already have the customer, so there is no additional cost in acquiring him. Your task becomes one of getting him to come to you more often. Some suggestions as to how you can do this follow.

Your Attitude and That of Your Employees

You need to make your customers feel comfortable when they deal with you. A friendly, efficient service will help them make a decision to return to you. If they feel unwelcome they are likely to try somewhere else next time they buy. There are few things more damaging to your business than treating your customers as if you don't care. Simply acknowledging your customers may be the difference between keeping or losing them. Make dealing with you a pleasant experience.

Saying Thank You

There are few more powerful words in our language than a genuine 'thank you'. Why not use it as part of your campaign to have people buy more often from you? Let them know you appreciate them doing business with you. Why not write a letter to your customers after making a sale, thanking them for their custom? If you do that, they are most likely to return next time they need the service or product you have provided.

Providing Information

Look at your product knowledge and your willingness to share it with your customers. Let them know of the services and other products you can provide. Let them know how they can use these products or services to their benefit. Take the time to explain how a product works.

Communicate With Your Customers

Your customers may not be aware that you can provide something they have been buying elsewhere. It is important that you keep in touch with them and keep them informed of offers, promotions and benefits that your business can provide them. Direct mailings, newsletters, or brochures are a means of achieving this.

REVIEW YOUR GROSS MARGINS

Your gross margin shows the proportion of turnover that is retained as gross profit. Gross profit is the difference between the price you charge for the goods you sell and the price you pay for them. Your gross margin is calculated by dividing your gross profit into your sales. You can only increase your gross profit percentage by:

➠ Raising your prices; or

➠ Buying or manufacturing your stock at a lower price.

You need to be aware, as part of your planning process, of what is an acceptable gross profit margin for the business you are in. Reference to the FMRC Benchmarks will help in this regard.

You also need to be aware of your product mix. The gross margin in your profit and loss account is a consolidation of the margins of all the products that you deal in. Some of these may be satisfactory; others not. For this reason you need to calculate the gross margin for each of your product lines. Those that do not meet your targets should be dropped, providing it is not necessary to stock them to sell other more profitable items, or unless they are being used as loss-leaders (products which sell at a loss but which help the sale of other products). You should ask yourself what effect dropping a particular product would have on your profit.

REVIEW YOUR FIXED COSTS

Fixed costs are those costs that remain the same regardless of sales volume. These include your rent, insurance, and most of your overheads. They are different from your variable costs, which are costs that increase or decrease according to turnover. These include sales commission and delivery expenses.

One way of keeping focused on your fixed costs is to ask yourself how many extra sales will be necessary to pay for proposed expenditure. If you sell an item for $10 and that product costs you $5, you will need to sell ten of those items to pay for expenditure of $50. If you incur the expenditure and only sell five of them, your net profit will be reduced by $25.

The review of what you do in your business, and the removal of those things that are unnecessary, may lead to a reduction in fixed costs. Overheads should be monitored closely and wastage removed.

PROFIT IMPROVEMENT WORKSHEET

	% Now	% Budgeted

Customer Base

No. of Customers at Start of Yr ....

Add Customers Gained Each Yr ....

Deduct Customers Lost Each Yr ....

Customer Base .... **A**

Sales Frequency

No. of Times Customers Buy
From You per Yr .... **B**

No. of Sales per Customer per Yr .... **C** =
A x **B**

Turnover

Average Sale Value .... **D**

Turnover .... **E** =
C x **D**

Profitability

Gross Profit Margin .... **F**

Gross Profit .... **G** =
E x **F**

Expenses .... **H**

Net Profit .... **G** - **H**

Profit Improvement

Budgeted Net Profit ....

Net Profit Now ....

Budgeted Improvement ....

BUDGETING

CASH FLOW, SALES, PROFIT AND LOSS ACCOUNTS AND BALANCE SHEETS

"We need to prepare some budgets," I said. "It is important that these be realistic, and that we monitor performance against our projections each month and amend them as time goes by. We have already started by doing the calculations when we looked at growing your business, but it is time to take this a little further."

"It's about time you got down to some real accountant's work," Jim said mock-seriously, grinning from ear to ear like a Cheshire cat.

"I'll pretend I didn't hear that," I replied. "I thought real accountant's work was what we have been doing all day. The days of an accountant being a bean counter are long gone, at least for me they are."

"Let's start with your profit and loss projections. You saw the effect on profit that certain strategies can have, when we went through the ways you can grow your business. We will incorporate some of those into the projections."

After some discussion we prepared a profit and loss projection for the next 12 months (shown overleaf), drawn up to account for the measures which were to be implemented as a result of the plan. After analysing Jim and Marney's collection and payment history we then compiled a cash flow projection (set out on pages 117 to 119).

JIM'S CAR CARE CENTRE PROFIT AND LOSS PROJECTION

	1999						2000						YEAR
	July	Aug	Sept	Oct	Nov	Dec	Jan	Feb	March	April	May	June	
Sales	76000	80000	72000	62000	76000	80000	60000	68000	80000	76000	80000	80000	890000
Less Cost of Goods Sold													
Opening Stock	29640	29640	29640	29640	29640	29640	29640	29640	29640	29640	29640	29640	29640
Purchases	37240	39200	35280	30380	37240	39200	29400	33320	39200	37240	39200	39200	436100
	66880	68840	64920	60020	66880	68840	59040	62960	68840	66880	68840	68840	465740
Closing Stock	29640	29640	29640	29640	29640	29640	29640	29640	29640	29640	29640	29640	29640
	37240	39200	35280	30380	37240	39200	29400	33320	39200	37240	39200	39200	436100
Gross Profit	38760	40800	36720	31620	38760	40800	30600	34680	40800	38760	40800	40800	453900
Expenses													
Accountancy	400	1200	400	400	400	400	400	400	400	400	400	400	5600
Advertising	3400	3400	3400	3400	3400	3400	3400	3400	3400	3400	3400	3400	40800
Bank Charges	490	490	490	490	490	490	490	490	490	490	490	490	5880
Cleaning	80	80	80	80	80	80	80	80	80	80	80	80	960

JIM'S CAR CARE CENTRE PROFIT AND LOSS PROJECTION (Cont'd)

| | 1999 | | | | | 2000 | | | | | | | |
	July	Aug	Sept	Oct	Nov	Dec	Jan	Feb	March	April	May	June	YEAR
Credit Card Charges	304	320	288	248	304	320	240	272	320	304	320	320	3560
Depreciation	980	980	980	980	980	980	980	980	980	980	980	980	11760
Donations	20	20	20	20	20	20	20	20	20	20	20	20	240
Entertainment	70	70	70	70	70	70	70	70	70	70	70	70	840
Freight & Cartage	304	320	288	248	304	320	240	272	320	304	320	320	3560
Hire of Pl. & Equip.	30	30	30	30	30	30	30	30	30	30	30	30	360
Insurance	0	0	1000	0	0	3400	0	0	0	0	0	0	4400
Interest	424	424	367	329	275	240	244	218	167	157	157	157	3159
Light & Power	0	800	0	0	800	0	0	800	0	0	800	0	3200
Motor Running	1660	1660	1660	1660	1660	1660	1660	1660	1660	1660	1660	1660	19920
Permits & Fees	60	60	60	60	60	60	60	60	60	60	60	60	720
Postage	80	80	80	80	80	80	80	80	80	80	80	80	960
Printing & Stationery	600	200	310	400	200	400	900	200	200	300	210	320	4240

JIM'S CAR CARE CENTRE PROFIT AND LOSS PROJECTION (Cont'd)

	1999						2000						YEAR
	July	Aug	Sept	Oct	Nov	Dec	Jan	Feb	March	April	May	June	
Registration Fees	400	0	0	0	300	0	0	0	400	0	0	0	1100
Rent	2400	2400	2400	2400	2400	2400	2400	2400	2400	2400	2400	2400	28800
Repairs & Maintenance	360	360	360	360	360	360	360	360	360	360	360	360	4320
Security	190	190	190	190	190	190	190	190	190	190	190	190	2280
Staff & Customer Amenities	456	480	432	372	456	480	360	408	480	456	480	480	5340
Subscriptions	80	80	80	80	80	80	80	80	80	80	80	80	960
Superannuation	1288	1288	1288	1288	1288	1288	1288	1288	1288	1288	1288	1288	15456
Telephone	600	600	600	600	600	600	600	600	600	600	600	600	7200
Tool Replacem't	60	60	60	60	60	60	60	60	60	60	60	60	720
Wages	18400	18400	18400	18400	18400	18400	18400	18400	18400	18400	18400	18400	220800
Workshop Supplies	274	288	259	223	274	288	216	245	288	274	288	288	3205
	33410	34280	33592	32468	33561	36096	32848	33063	32823	32443	33223	32533	400340
Net Profit	5350	6520	3128	-848	5199	4704	-2248	1617	7977	6317	7577	8267	53560

JIM'S CAR CARE CENTRE CASH FLOW PROJECTION

	1999	2000											YEAR
	Jul	Aug	Sep	Oct	Nov	Dec	Jan	Feb	Mar	Apr	May	Jun	
Opening Balance	-40000	-31857	-26483	-18595	-13701	-14578	-11029	-2616	-4128	-1254	7856	14286	-40000
Receipts													
Sales	80000	76000	80000	72000	62000	76000	80000	60000	68000	80000	76000	80000	890000
	40000	44143	53517	53405	48299	61422	68971	57384	63872	78746	83856	94286	850000
Payments													
Accountancy	400	1200	400	400	400	400	400	400	400	400	400	400	5600
Advertising	3400	3400	3400	3400	3400	3400	3400	3400	3400	3400	3400	3400	40800
Bank Charges	490	490	490	490	490	490	490	490	490	490	490	490	5880
Cleaning	80	80	80	80	80	80	80	80	80	80	80	80	960
Credit Card Charges	320	304	320	288	248	304	320	240	272	320	304	320	3560
Donations	20	20	20	20	20	20	20	20	20	20	20	20	240
Entertainment	70	70	70	70	70	70	70	70	70	70	70	70	840
Freight & Cartage	320	304	320	288	248	304	320	240	272	320	304	320	3560

JIM'S CAR CARE CENTRE CASH FLOW PROJECTION (Cont'd)

	1999					2000							
	Jul	Aug	Sep	Oct	Nov	Dec	Jan	Feb	Mar	Apr	May	Jun	YEAR
Hire of Pl. & Equip.	30	30	30	30	30	30	30	30	30	30	30	30	360
Insurance	0	0	1000	0	0	3400	0	0	0	0	0	0	4400
Interest	267	267	212	177	124	91	97	74	28	0	0	0	1336
Light & Power	0	800	0	0	800	0	0	800	0	0	800	0	3200
Loans	314	314	314	314	314	314	314	314	314	314	314	314	3768
Motor Running	1660	1660	1660	1660	1660	1660	1660	1660	1660	1660	1660	1660	19920
Permits & Fees	60	60	60	60	60	60	60	60	60	60	60	60	720
Postage	80	80	80	80	80	80	80	80	80	80	80	80	960
Printing & Stationery	600	200	310	400	200	400	900	200	200	300	210	320	4240
Purchases	39200	37240	39200	35280	30380	37240	39200	29400	33320	39200	37240	39200	436100
Registration Fees	400	0	0	0	300	0	0	0	400	0	0	0	1100
Rent	2400	2400	2400	2400	2400	2400	2400	2400	2400	2400	2400	2400	28800
Repairs & Maintenance	360	360	360	360	360	360	360	360	360	360	360	360	4320

JIM'S CAR CARE CENTRE CASH FLOW PROJECTION (Cont'd)

	1999						2000						YEAR
	Jul	Aug	Sep	Oct	Nov	Dec	Jan	Feb	Mar	Apr	May	Jun	
Security	190	190	190	190	190	190	190	190	190	190	190	190	2280
Staff & Customer Amenities	480	456	480	432	372	456	480	360	408	480	456	480	5340
Subscriptions	80	80	80	80	80	80	80	80	80	80	80	80	960
Superannuation	1288	1288	1288	1288	1288	1288	1288	1288	1288	1288	1288	1288	15456
Telephone	600	600	600	600	600	600	600	600	600	600	600	600	7200
Tool Replacem't	60	60	60	60	60	60	60	60	60	60	60	60	720
Wages	18400	18400	18400	18400	18400	18400	18400	18400	18400	18400	18400	18400	220800
Workshop Supplies	288	274	288	259	223	274	288	216	245	288	274	288	3204
	71857	70627	72112	67106	62877	72451	71587	61512	65127	70890	69570	70910	826624
Closing Balance	-31857	-26483	-18595	-13701	-14578	-11029	-2616	-4128	-1254	7856	14286	23376	23376

We then prepared a projected balance sheet as at 30 June 2000. The improvement in the gearing situation is the result of the policy to stop drawing profit from the business.

PROJECTED BALANCE SHEET

Current Assets	$
Cash on Hand	310
Cash at Bank	23,376
Inventory	29,640
Sundry Debtors	13,000
Other Current Assets	1,200
	67,526
Non-Current Assets	
Plant & Equipment	58,960
	126,486
Current Liabilities	
Creditors	54,133
Borrowings	3,768
	57,901
Non-Current Liabilities	
Borrowings	13,164
	13,164
Total Liabilities	71,065
Net Assets	55,421
Owners' Equity	$55,421

* * * * *

KEY POINTS

☞ Profit and loss projections and cash flows should be prepared and broken up into months.

☞ Balance sheet projections should be prepared on an annual basis.

☞ The budgets should be realistic.

☞ Budgeting is an ongoing process requiring monitoring and revision.

Budgets are a numerical expression of the planning process and quantify operating performance for the periods they cover. The plan outlines the objectives, which, if you are honest with yourself, are probably geared to creating wealth within the business. It articulates the details required and the strategies put in place to achieve that wealth. Planning is the process of deciding what the business is going to do and how it is going to do it. The budget can be viewed as being the focal point of the planning process. It provides you with a tool which you can use to monitor the operating and profit performance of your business by comparing the actual results against the targets. Budgeting is the financial evaluation of the plan.

THE ADVANTAGES OF BUDGETING

Some of the important functions of a budget are as follows:

❱ It provides a performance template which quantifies the financial implications of the business plan

- It results in a determination of the funds needed to operate the business

- It provides target figures against which actual results may be compared

- When compared to actual results, it highlights variances that need to be investigated

- It can alert you to potential problems

- It assists with the co-ordination of the activities of the business and ensures they are directed towards your strategic goal.

The minimum budgets needed in the business planning process are:

- The sales budget

- The profit and loss budget

- The balance sheet projection and

- The cash flow statement

These are discussed below.

THE SALES BUDGET

The sales budget should be the starting point in the preparation of financial projections. This is because turnover influences so many of the parts of the other budgets. Sales activity affects not only the profit and loss statement, balance sheet and cash flows, but the funding requirements, inventory levels, staff requirements, capital expenditure and the business viability. Some would argue that, for this reason, the sales budget is the most important budget you can prepare. There is no disputing the sales budget is significant, and should be prepared, but I remain to be convinced that other budgets are less important.

I have often experienced client resistance to the preparation of sales budgets. They have argued that it is not possible to forecast turnover with accuracy. Although there is truth in their reasoning, they are missing the point that their businesses rely on the selling of either goods or services and that it is impossible to plan without some idea as to their future turnover.

There are two types of costs:

1. *Variable* costs, which vary according to the level of turnover; and

2. *Fixed* costs, which are incurred no matter what the level of turnover.

If you don't prepare sales estimates, you cannot prepare estimates of your variable costs.

How to Prepare a Sales Budget

The sales forecast should be prepared on the basis of where you are heading rather than where you have been. By this I mean that you should not simply adjust the sales from the past by an indexation factor. The figures from the past report past achievements, not future possibilities. This having been said, the historical sales figures should be used as the starting point and then adjusted up and down to reflect:

➠ The current state of the economy

➠ The size of the market

➠ The expected growth or decline in sales in your market sector

➠ The activity of your competitors

➠ Changes in customer buying habits

➠ The expected growth or decline in your market share

➠ Your marketing strategies and the ability of your employees to carry them out successfully

➠ Your capacity to finance the expected turnover

➠ Technological developments.

It is important to ensure that your sales projections are achievable and realistic. If they are not, the rest of your planning will be inaccurate. The Department of Industry, Technology and Commerce booklet *Financial Budgeting in Small Business* summarises the need for realism succinctly when it says, "Forecasts must be based on what you can and will do and not upon what you would like or hope to do."

Some would argue that 'zero cost' budgeting should be used. This means that you should estimate your sales from base of zero. I suggest that it is far more practical to commence with your monthly sales data from the previous year. Take the unit sales for each month and adjust them up or down to reflect current market conditions. Then multiply your projections by your current prices. This should be done for individual products or services, product groups and customer groups. Sub-budgets should be prepared for geographical sales areas, customer types, and sales persons.

The sales budget should show total sales in both volume and value. You should understand, though, that high volume will not necessarily result in high profits.

EXAMPLE

Your business has two products. Product A sells for $40, and product B sells for $60. After reviewing your sales history and adjusting for the factors listed above you estimate unit sales as follows:

Month	Product A	Product B
July	1,000	300
August	1,200	600
September	800	500

These are entered into the budget as shown below and multiplied by the sale price to estimate the sales dollars.

	July	August	September
Product A			
Units	1,000	1,200	800
Price	40	40	40
Sales	40,000	48,000	32,000
Product B			
Units	300	600	500
Price	60	60	60
Sales	18,000	36,000	30,000
Total	**$58,000**	**$84,000**	**$62,000**

THE PROFIT AND LOSS BUDGET

The profit and loss account discloses results for the period reported on. It helps explain the changes that have occurred in your equity in your business between the beginning and end of that period. It measures the surplus or deficit of income over expenditure for the period it covers. Normally it will be prepared using the accrual basis of accounting. This means that income is recognised when it is earned rather than when you receive it, and expenses are recognised when they are incurred rather than when you pay for them. It may be set out as:

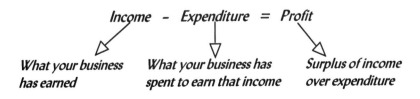

Income - Expenditure = Profit

What your business has earned   *What your business has spent to earn that income*   *Surplus of income over expenditure*

125

Or in the form of a trading, profit & loss statement:

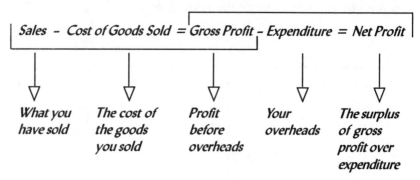

Sales	–	Cost of Goods Sold	= Gross Profit	–	Expenditure	= Net Profit

| What you have sold | The cost of the goods you sold | Profit before overheads | Your overheads | The surplus of gross profit over expenditure |

The profit and loss budget brings together the figures gathered from the sales, purchases and expense budgets and shows the expected income, expenditure and profit for the period concerned. It should disclose the estimated:

➡ Turnover;

➡ Cost of goods sold;

➡ Gross profit;

➡ Expenses; and

➡ Net profit.

THE BALANCE SHEET PROJECTION

What is a Balance Sheet?

Your balance sheet shows the financial position of your business as at the date it is prepared. It shows what you own, what you owe and what you have invested in your business – that is, your business assets, liabilities and equity. It does not show what your business is worth. Unless otherwise stated, items are shown at historical cost. Their current value is ignored. Unfortunately it is full of technical terms. Take its name, for instance, the balance sheet. Perhaps we should rename it a 'statement of finance and investment'. This is because it is a report on how the business is financed and where the money has been invested.

How the business is financed:

$$Equity \ = \ the \ owner's \ investment$$

$$Debt \ = \ money \ owed \ to \ other \ people$$

How the money is invested:

$$Assets \ = \ what \ the \ business \ owns$$

How the business is financed must equal how the money is invested:

$$Equity \ + \ Debt \ = \ Assets$$

Or, as often stated:

$$Equity \ = \ Assets \ - \ Debt$$

EQUITY

Equity will be shown as one of the following:

➠ Shareholders' funds;

➠ Partners' funds;

➠ Proprietorship;

➠ Trust funds; or

➠ Equity

depending on the legal structure of your business.

ASSETS

A balance sheet will normally group assets under two headings:

1. Current assets; and

2. Non-current assets.

Current Assets

Current assets are assets that would normally be used or converted into cash within a year. These may include (amongst other things):

➡ Cash

➡ Debtors (what is owed to you by others)

➡ Stock.

Non-Current Assets

Non-current assets are more permanent assets which would normally be held for longer than one year, such as:

➡ Plant and equipment

➡ Land and buildings.

DEBT

Debt will normally be categorised as:

1. Current liabilities; and
2. Non-current liabilities.

Current Liabilities

Current liabilities are debts which you would normally expect to repay within one year. These may include:

➡ Bank overdrafts

➡ Creditors (what you owe your suppliers)

➡ Loans

➡ Provisions (amounts provided for holiday pay, income tax, etc.).

Non-Current Liabilities

Non-current liabilities are debts which are not classified as current liabilities, such as the portion of loans that will not be repaid within 12 months.

THE BALANCE SHEET BUDGET

The balance sheet budget is an estimate of your assets and liabilities during the planning period.

There is little point in preparing a balance sheet projection on a monthly basis. Normally it is sufficient to prepare it on an annual basis, commencing from the start of the first year of the business plan and for the end of each year for the period covered by the plan.

A review of the balance sheet projections will reveal:

➠ Whether the plan results in a growth or decline in assets

➠ The gearing being utilised and any need for additional capital

➠ The liquidity and its soundness

➠ The inventory levels

➠ The working capital

➠ Whether there is a need for capital expenditure

➠ Where the money which has come into the business has gone, and where it has come from.

CASH FLOW STATEMENTS

Often when a bank manager asks you for a business plan, what he is really asking for is a cash flow statement. He is concerned with the ability of your business to meet its financial commitments. More particularly, he wants to satisfy himself whether and when the bank is likely to get its money back. That is a legitimate request but should not be the reason for preparing a cash flow statement. A cash flow statement should form an integral part of the management budgetary procedures in the normal course of business.

What is a Cash Flow Statement?

A cash flow statement shows how much money is flowing into a business and how much is flowing out. It is normally prepared on a monthly basis. In contrast, a profit and loss projection shows the estimated income which it matches against the estimated expenses. This results in a projected profit or loss.

The timing of the receipt of income and the payment of expenses will result in a difference between the two sets of figures, even if the only receipts are income and the only payments are expenses. A business may sell goods in one month and get paid for them in another. Similarly, it may incur expenditure in one month and not pay for it until another.

Not all money received will be income – loans, receipts for sale of plant and equipment, and capital injected into a business are examples of this. These would not be recorded in a profit and loss projection, but are part of a cash flow statement. Payments made for capital items, such as new machinery, drawings, investments, and loan repayments are recorded in the cash flow statement but have no place in the profit and loss projection. These are balance sheet items. Non-cash expenses such as depreciation form part of a profit and loss projection but have no place in a cash flow statement.

A business may be trading profitably, but beyond its financial capacity. Its sales grow and with it the need to finance its debtors and stock on hand. At the same time, the amounts it has to pay its suppliers increase. Eventually, if that growth occurs too quickly, the business finds itself under-funded and in trouble. This is called over-trading and has resulted in financial disaster for many profitable businesses. The preparation of cash flow budgets can forewarn of the approaching disaster.

It has been written (in *How to Prepare a Business Plan* by Edward Blackwell) that the primary purpose of a cash flow forecast is to persuade the bank or other institution to lend you the money you need. I strongly disagree. The primary purpose of a cash flow forecast is the provision of a management tool that forewarns of cash surpluses and deficiencies so that they can be managed efficiently.

The Advantages of Preparing Cash Flow Statements

Cash flow statements are useful because of their ability to:

‣ Forecast cash surpluses

‣ Forecast cash deficits

‣ Indicate your monthly cash requirements and help you make adequate provision

‣ Alert you to the need for long-term financing

‣ Signal a need for an improvement in the collection of accounts receivable

‣ Highlight a tendency to overtrade

‣ Assist a lender in assessing your ability to meet the loan requirements

‣ Force you to consider the cash implications of running the business.

Disadvantages of Preparing Cash Flow Statements

Possible disadvantages include the following:

‣ A poorly prepared and inaccurate cash forecast could lead to a finance application being refused

‣ Inaccurate projections may result in poor decision-making.

Objections Raised to Preparing Cash Flow Statements

It is common for small business owners and operators to query the worth of preparing cash flow statements on the basis that they believe it is impossible to predict when money will flow in. This indicates a lack of understanding of the purpose of the tool. All budgeting involves estimating. By referring to past data it is possible to make objective forward projections. These do not have to be accurate to the dollar. If things turn out differently to your expectations, answers should be sought to explain the divergences, whether they be favourable or otherwise. You will find that the more experience you gain in preparing cash flow statements, the more accurate they will become.

How do You Prepare a Cash Flow Statement?

Step One – The Opening Balance

It is normal to prepare a cash flow statement which covers a 12-month period. The projection is usually broken up into monthly columns. You begin with your bank balance at the start of the cash flow period, that is, the balance of your reconciled cash book. Most times this will be different from your bank statement balance. This is because there will usually be cheques that have been drawn that have not yet been presented. As well, you may have cash you have received and have not yet banked but which you have included in your cash book.

Step Two – The Receipts

The first monthly receipt to consider is your sales or, if you are in a service industry, your fees. To make this easier it may pay to break this figure into two parts: cash sales and account sales. Past experience will tell what percentage of your turnover is from cash sales. You will get your cash sales figure by multiplying your estimated sales for the month by that percentage. Your estimated sales are taken from the sales budget, which should have been prepared prior to the cash flow budget. Subtracting this cash sales figure from your estimated sales will give your account sales.

EXAMPLE

Total Annual Sales	$600,000
Annual Cash Sales	$240,000
Cash Sales/Total Sales = 40%	
Account Sales = 100% − 40%	
= 60%	
Estimated Sales for the Month	$70,000
Cash Sales	$28,000
Account Sales	$42,000

You can estimate your receipt of the account sales by referring to your credit terms and the degree of customer compliance with those terms. If you offer 30 days credit and half of your customers observe these terms, 50% of your account sales will be received in the month following the sale. If a further 40% pay in the following month then 40% of your sales will be received in the second month after it is made. If the remaining 10% pay in 90 days then the cash for those sales will not be received until three months after the sale. Reference to your monthly debtors aged trial balance will help you calculate these percentages. This information will help you calculate the monthly receipt of account sales. You will also need to allow for discounts given and any bad debts incurred.

EXAMPLE

Let us assume that you have chosen the month of September past as being indicative of a normal trading month. Your analysis reveals:

Account Sales for September $80,000

These were collected as follows:

	$	%
October	40,000	50
November	32,000	40
December	8,000	10

You would calculate your estimated debtors collection for the month of October as follows:

Month of Sale	Credit Sales ($)	Collection	$
July	$42,000	10%	4,200
August	$58,000	40%	23,200
September	$80,000	50%	40,000
October Receipts			$67,400

In October, based on the past, you would expect your collections to be made up of:

⇒   10% of July sales;

⇒   40% of August sales; and

⇒   50% of September sales.

In reality, some of October's account sales would be paid in October. This has been ignored to keep the example simple.

In this example you would include $67,400 as your credit sales figure in your cash flow projection.

A more scientific means of calculating the collection of credit sales would be to use regression analysis. This is a statistical method used to estimate the relationship between a dependent variable and one or more independent variables and to predict, using linear regression, a future value. Discussion of this method is beyond the scope of this book.

You then need to consider other non-sales receipts that may be banked in the budgetary period. These may include loans, monies for sale of assets, capital injected into the business, or rebates received, amongst other things. These should be allocated to the month of expected receipt.

Step Three – The Payments

The cash outflow of a business is measured by the payments made. So you need to review your projected expenditure and allocate it according to the month you expect to make the payment, rather than the month you expect to incur it. You shouldn't take your annual expenditure and divide the components by twelve. This will not reflect reality. For example, purchases of your trading stock will reflect your sales pattern and vary from month to month. Payments for these will be determined by the credit terms you are granted by your suppliers and the availability of cash to meet your commitment. Some expenses, such as rent, will be a constant figure each month. Others will be paid for in some months and not in others. An example is insurance. There may only be one or two months in the year when you make a payment for this expense. These irregular expenses should be allocated to the month you expect them to be paid.

Purchase of Goods for Resale

A method of allocating your stock purchases is to take the estimated sales figure for a month (from the sales budget, not the cash flow projection) and multiply it by the percentage of cost of goods sold. This will give you the cost of purchase for that month. You should then allocate the payment based on the frequency you pay your creditors. For example, if you pay in 30 days you should allocate the payment to the month after making the purchase.

EXAMPLE

Estimated Sales $60,000

Gross Profit Percentage = 40%

Cost of Goods Sold = (100% − 40%) x $60,000

$$= 60\% \times \$60,000$$

$$= \$36,000$$

Purchase Terms = 30 days

Goods Purchased July

Payment in August

Your financial statement budget will allocate the $36,000 to July. It will be allocated to August in your cash flow projection.

Loan Interest

When preparing projected financial statements you need to differentiate between the interest and the principal component of loan repayments. That is not required when preparing a cash flow statement. The concern here is the loan payment, that is the amount being paid for the period being considered.

Overdraft Interest

For cash flow purposes, overdraft interest should be calculated as:

Closing balance for the month (from your cash flow budget)

x annual overdraft interest rate, then ÷ 365,

then x the figure by the days of the month concerned

Enter the final figure in the interest row in the column for the next month.

This is an approximation only because your overdraft will vary from day to day. It may be in credit for part of the month and debit in another. However, it is necessary to make an allowance for the expected cost.

Grouping of Expenses

The purpose of the cash flow statement is to estimate the cash situation at the end of each period in the projection. If prepared on a monthly basis you are projecting the monthly balances; if on a quarterly basis you are projecting quarterly balances. The focus should be on this end figure.

If you break up your payments into too many components it is possible to lose this focus. For this reason items such as motor running should be shown as one figure and not be broken up into subcategories such as registrations, insurance, fuel, leasing, and repairs. Detailed allocations should be maintained in worksheets, so they can be analysed separately if required. Similarly small items should be grouped together as sundries. Again, the components should be recorded in a separate worksheet that can be referred to if necessary.

An example of a cash flow statement prepared, on a monthly basis, for a three-month period is shown overleaf.

	Month 1	Month 2	Month 3
Opening Balance	10,000	10,500	8,600
Receipts			
Sales	70,000	74,000	72,000
Loans	0	20,000	0
	70,000	94,000	72,000
	80,000	104,500	80,600
Payments			
Purchases	56,000	60,000	57,000
Wages	5,000	6,000	5,700
Rent	1,800	1,800	1,800
Loan Repayments	1,200	1,200	1,200
Equipment	0	20,000	0
Drawings	3,000	4,000	2,000
Overheads	1,500	1,900	1,300
Other	1,000	1,000	2,000
	69,500	95,900	71,000
Closing Balance	$10,500	$8,600	$9,600

I set out cash flow statements in this way because I want to know the estimated cash balance at the end of each month. My primary concern is not the monthly flow, it is the result of the flow. An alternative presentation is set out opposite. For me this focuses on the flow rather than the result. Either method is acceptable. The important thing is that the statement be prepared.

	Month 1	Month 2	Month 3
Receipts			
Sales	70,000	74,000	72,000
Loans	0	20,000	0
	70,000	94,000	72,000
Payments			
Purchases	56,000	60,000	57,000
Wages	5,000	6,000	5,700
Rent	1,800	1,800	1,800
Loan Repayments	1,200	1,200	1,200
Equipment	0	20,000	0
Drawings	3,000	4,000	2,000
Overheads	1,500	1,900	1,300
Other	1,000	1,000	2,000
	69,500	95,900	71,000
Cash Flow	500	(1,900)	1,000
Opening Balance	10,000	10,500	8,600
Closing Balance	$10,500	$8,600	$9,600

This could be improved by changing the section below the cash flow as follows:

Opening Balance	10,000	10,500	8,600
Cash Flow	500	(1,900)	1,000
Closing Balance	$10,500	$8,600	$9,600

PREPARING THE ACTION PLAN

ACTION PLAN

"The time has come for us to get to the heart of the plan," I said, feeling the effects of what had been a long day.

"Everything we have done to this point was preparation. We have looked at your vision for your business and how to use your business to provide you with the lifestyle you desire. We have studied the nature of your business and its strengths and weaknesses. Your operations have been analysed and we have seen the effects that some fairly small changes can have on your profitability. We have discussed what is meant by your critical success factors and the need to measure them by identifying your key performance indicators. One important critical success factor has been identified and you have agreed to implement the steps to measure the achievement of that immediately. Finally, we have drafted some preliminary budgets to encompass the things we have talked about. But all of that is just the basis for the most important part of our project. We now need to prepare an action plan."

"That makes sense," said Marney.

"We have a list of the things that need to be done," I stated. "Now we need to prioritise them. We must set times for their completion and assign a responsibility to either of you or one of your staff to ensure that they are done."

"Let me give you an example," I continued. "After that we will call it a day. I want you to drop your completed action plan back to me at the office, next week. Then I will draw up a business plan which documents the thrust of our exercise. This will be *your* plan, not mine, because you have been involved in its preparation. I have been the facilitator in this process. You have done most of the work. I would prefer that you write the plan, and you will as you modify it in the future. But you need a precedent, and it will be quicker for me to do that for you."

"You have identified the need to implement measures to ensure that customers' cars are ready when promised," I said. "We agree that steps should be taken immediately to ensure that this goal is met and we identified some measures we could put in place to achieve this."

I handed Jim and Marney a pre-prepared sheet with the heading 'Action Plan'. I had made an entry as we had talked.

ACTION PLAN

No.	Action	Priority	Time for Completion	To be Done by	Resources Needed
1	Introduce a quality control system to ensure completion of jobs when promised to customers	Urgent	15 June 1999	Jim	Staff members

"I think we can do that," said Jim.

"I think we *need* to do that," emphasised Marney.

"I agree," I said, "but later. Time is getting on and we have got through far more today than I expected. Let's call it a day. We are almost there with this, yet this is only the beginning."

"We can see that," said Marney. "There are going to be a lot of changes."

"Yes," I agreed, "but over time. We have to introduce them gradually so as to minimise the disruption to your business."

"I am both angry and pleased," said Jim as we stood at the Watson's car.

"What do you mean?" I asked.

"You should have asked us to do this exercise a long time ago," Jim replied. "I am upset that you didn't. I understand that we probably wouldn't have wanted to do it anyway, but we should have been made aware that you could help us in this way. I am pleased that we agreed to this exercise. We have learned so much, and realised that we were working for a living, running our business from day to day without any real direction. We have been reacting to events as they have happened rather than preparing for them. We have not been managing our business."

"That is the case for the majority of small business people like yourselves," I said. "You are right. I should have made you aware of the need to plan a long time ago. We talked about the reasons for that early this morning. I am not going to make any excuses, but the important thing is that we have now knuckled down and done something about it."

With that Jim and Marney drove off. They had started the journey towards a more rewarding and enjoyable business future.

✻ ✻ ✻ ✻ ✻

> ### KEY POINTS
>
> ☛ The action plan is the core of your planning exercise – without it you do not have a plan.
>
> ☛ You should prepare the action plan yourself. That way you are establishing the priorities and taking responsibility for it.

The action plan is the key component of any business plan. After all, there is little use in undertaking an exercise to decide what you are going to do if you don't determine when you are going to do it. Yet that is precisely what a lot of business plans do. They do not include an action plan. After you have prepared the action plan, the rest of it is just back-up, a record as to how you determined the plan you are going to implement. The reality is that everything done in the business planning exercise should be being done so that a plan for action can be prepared. The plan must be consistent with your objectives and strategies. That is, it must assign to each item you have researched in the plan:

⇒ A priority

⇒ A time by which it must be done

⇒ An allocation of responsibility for ensuring that it is done

⇒ The resources that are required for doing it.

PRIORITY

You should rank the things that have to be done according to their level of importance. The ranking be consistent with the achievement of your financial forecasts. Those actions that have a major effect on the changes that need to be made to meet your goals should be attended to first. It is human nature to do the easiest things first and leave the hard things till later. Often the hard things never get done. These may be the very things that need to be attended to, in order to achieve the aims of your plan.

TIMING

Each action should be allocated a time for completion. This should be realistic and in line with your overall plan. You need to follow up to ensure that the action steps are being implemented within the time frame laid down. Failure to do so may undermine the plan.

RESPONSIBILITY

You need to allocate responsibility for ensuring that the action step is done. Most likely, in small business that responsibility will be yours. But there may be some tasks that can be delegated to your employees. Whether it be yourself, your partner or an employee, allocate the responsibility and follow up to ensure it is being done.

REQUIRED RESOURCES

There may be items that have to be purchased in order to implement the action, for example a computer. There may be things that have to be done in conjunction with others, or there may be information that needs to be gathered before the action can be attended to. These are the resources required. It is important to realise that each action must be possible with the resources you have or are able to obtain.

A format for an action plan is presented opposite.

ACTION PLAN

No.	Action	Priority	Time for Completion	To be Done by	Resources Needed
1	....	....	....	....	....
2	....	....	....	....	....
3	....	....	....	....	....
4	....	....	....	....	....
5	....	....	....	....	....
6	....	....	....	....	....
7	....	....	....	....	....
8	....	....	....	....	....
9	....	....	....	....	....
10	....	....	....	....	....

OTHER ACTION PLANS

These actions should be viewed as paths toward your business goals. That is, they are the things that need to be done to ensure your business ends up where you want it to be in the future. They can be broken up into sub-plans. For example, in *Your Own Business: A Practical Guide to Success*, Wal Reynolds, Warwick Savage and Alan Williams discuss writing your working plans. They say that "the main working plans are for:

➡ Work flow;

➡ Staff;

➠   Information; and

➠   Control."

Work Flow

Work flow involves the processing of goods and services, that is, the manufacturing of goods, the provision of services, the purchasing of goods for resale and the selling of those goods to your customers. It covers the things you need to implement to ensure the orderly distribution of your goods or services and to reach your target market.

Staff

The staff action plan involves the changes you need to implement in respect of your staffing levels, staff selection, training, responsibilities and duties. It also involves your future staff needs and the actions you need to take to ensure your employees work together towards the achievement of your goals.

Information

This plan attends to the changes you need to make to ensure that the information necessary for the business to function is recorded, stored and used.

Control

The control plan includes the actions that need to be implemented to measure performance against budgets, put in place appropriate policies and procedures and provide warning signs when things are not going to plan.

CO-OPERATION

The action plan will need the co-operation of your staff. In some instances they will be responsible for attending to the actions that need to be done to put your plan into practice. For this reason they must be aware of the plan and what you are trying to achieve. The implications of the actions that affect their job must be explained to them. It is important that they understand why, so that they work with you in ensuring the goals you have set are met.

ADAPTABILITY

The plan should not be cast in stone. Conditions may change, and unforeseen events can occur. New competitors may enter the marketplace, costs may rise, or consumer spending may fall. These and other things do occur. When this happens it may be necessary to revise the plan. You should not just continue on as if nothing has happened. It may be that the changes are so significant, the plan may have to be rewritten in full.

WRITING THE PLAN

 A SAMPLE PLAN

A week later I handed Jim and Marney their completed plan. This was their plan, a plan they had formulated by going through the steps I had outlined. The plan is set out in the following pages.

JIM'S CAR CARE CENTRE BUSINESS PLAN
Prepared for James and Marney Watson on 18 May 1999

Introduction

This business plan has been prepared as a working document to be used to measure the progress and direct the focus of the business known as Jim's Car Care Centre towards the objectives established by its owners.

The plans and objectives outlined in this plan may change over time. As the business develops there will be a need to respond to various market forces over which the owners have no control. For this reason modifications will be needed as time progresses.

The plan provides its owners with a map for the future. It is a tool to help them measure the extent to which they are staying on the path they have laid down for the years ahead.

The plan includes their expectations for their business over the next five years.

An Overview of the Business

Jim's Car Care Centre was established as a partnership between James and Marney Watson in 1994 to provide a specialist steering and suspension service to the general public. The partners have identified a significant market in Brisbane for the sale of its products and services. Within this market there is significant competition. The major competitor, GT's Suspension Centres, has a chain of workshops located throughout Brisbane.

The business operates from a 3,500 square foot warehouse on the Pacific Highway, Springwood, Queensland. It employs seven people – the two partners, a service manager, three mechanics, and an apprentice.

The Owners' Vision for the Business

The partners plan to expand the business by opening two stores within the next five years. These stores are to be located on the Gold Coast and on the Brisbane Northside.

The primary objective of the owners is to develop a profitable business which will enable them to enjoy a comfortable lifestyle.

The Key Expectations of the Customers

The owners recognise that the three key expectations of their customers are: quality, price and service. With this in mind they will seek to develop the resources and procedures necessary to meet these expectations and grow their position in the marketplace.

The Five-Year Plan Summary

1999/2000	— Identify the key performance indicators of the business
	— Measure the key performance indicators
	— Attend to monthly reviews of financial projections
	— Systemise procedures
	— Set up customer focus groups
2000/2001	— Continue the development of systems within the business
	— Cosolidate operations
	— Review objectives
2001/2002	— Open a store on the Northside
	— Appoint a manager for Springwood
	— Review objectives
	— Pay a dividend
2002/2003	— Review the systems and procedures to ensure they are still adequate for the business
	— Consolidate the business
	— Review objectives
2003/2004	— Appoint a general manager so as to allow for more leisure time away from the business
	— Review objectives
	— Open a store on the Gold Coast

The five-year business plan for Jim's Car Care Centre is summarised above. The owners recognise that the business is in an early stage of its development cycle. A series of steps have been formulated to enable the business to meet the vision the owners have for it in the next five years.

1999/2000

There is a need to commence extensive systems and procedural development work. A number of steps need to be taken to put in place systems which measure those things that are necessary for the business to succeed. This includes the identification of key performance indicators that, once identified, are to be measured and reviewed on a weekly basis. Initial profit and loss, cash flow and balance sheet projections have been prepared and are set out later in this report (see pages 154-160). These are to be reviewed regularly and amended as necessary. The cash flow budget is to be extended monthly so that there is always a 12-month forecast in place.

It is recognised that an important method of obtaining feedback about what the customers require from the business, and therefore what must be done for the business to enjoy an extended period of growth, is the establishment of customer focus groups. Consequently, the top six customers are to be invited to an evening where, as well as being given refreshments, they will be asked to tell the owners what they want from the business, how well their needs are being served, the things that they perceive the business to be doing well and those things they don't like about doing business with Jim's Car Care Centre.

It is intended that these meetings be held once every three months, with a different group of customers being invited to each meeting so that a range of views can be heard.

2000/2001

By this time a significant amount of work will have been completed on systems and procedural development. This will continue until its completion later in this year.

Steps will be taken to develop an extended product range to provide a greater range to the market than currently being provided. This will lead to the creation of a system to achieve a recurring income base for the business.

At the end of this year the vision and objectives of the owners will be reviewed to see if their focus and ideas have changed. The business plan will be adapted to ensure it is in line with these.

The owners will begin to look for a suitable site for a workshop on the Northside of Brisbane. This will broaden the market area served by the business, which to date has been south of the Brisbane river.

2001/2002

A workshop will be opened north of the Brisbane river. This is planned to occur in the first quarter of the income year. This will be funded by borrowings and funds retained in the business from the growth and improved profitability that will have been experienced over the past two years. An exercise comparing the benefits of leasing to purchasing will be undertaken and the decision as to how to finance the new equipment will be based on the findings of the study.

A manager will be appointed towards the end of the year for the Springwood workshop. It is envisaged that the owners' time will be spent overseeing both stores. By this time the owners should be able to reduce the hours they are actively involved in the business and plan to use that time looking at other opportunities that may arise.

A dividend is planned to be paid in this year. The owners will have forgone any drawings other than their wages for the past two years so as to overcome a gearing problem that had occurred from their drawing all profits from the business. It is envisaged, from the projections made, that this will be able to be done without placing any strain on the business's working capital.

2002/2003

The 2002/2003 income year will be one of consolidation. Systems and procedures will be reviewed to ensure they are still adequate for the business. Considerable growth will have occurred and the objectives of the owners will be reviewed to ensure that the business is still progressing in accord with their long-term goals. A suitable location will be sought on the Gold Coast to open a third workshop early in the next financial year.

2003/2004

A workshop will be opened on the Gold Coast, spreading the geographic area served by the business. Profitability should be such that a general manager will be able to be appointed, enabling the owners to have more leisure time and pursue other personal interests. The business will now be in a mature state. A detailed review will be undertaken to ensure that the systems are able to cope with the growth. Consideration will be given to the possibility of franchising the business concept.

FINANCIAL PROJECTIONS

Annual Profit and Loss Budget Summary

	2000	2001	2002	2003	2004
Sales	890,000	1,200,000	1,700,000	2,300,000	3,000,000
Gross Profit	453,900	612,000	867,000	1,173,000	1,530,000
Expenditure	400,339	540,000	720,000	850,000	1,200,000
Net Profit*	$53,561	72,000	147,000	323,000	330,000

*After owners' remuneration

Monthly Profit And Loss Summary

This is shown on pages 154 to 156.

Cash Flow Projection for the Year Ending 30 June 2000

This is shown on pages 157 to 159.

JIM'S CAR CARE CENTRE PROFIT AND LOSS PROJECTION

	1999						2000						YEAR
	July	Aug	Sept	Oct	Nov	Dec	Jan	Feb	March	April	May	June	
Sales	76000	80000	72000	62000	76000	80000	60000	68000	80000	76000	80000	80000	890000
Less Cost of Goods Sold													
Opening Stock	29640	29640	29640	29640	29640	29640	29640	29640	29640	29640	29640	29640	29640
Purchases	37240	39200	35280	30380	37240	39200	29400	33320	39200	37240	39200	39200	436100
	66880	68840	64920	60020	66880	68840	59040	62960	68840	66880	68840	68840	465740
Closing Stock	29640	29640	29640	29640	29640	29640	29640	29640	29640	29640	29640	29640	29640
	37240	39200	35280	30380	37240	39200	29400	33320	39200	37240	39200	39200	436100
Gross Profit	38760	40800	36720	31620	38760	40800	30600	34680	40800	38760	40800	40800	453900
Expenses													
Accountancy	400	1200	400	400	400	400	400	400	400	400	400	400	5600
Advertising	3400	3400	3400	3400	3400	3400	3400	3400	3400	3400	3400	3400	40800
Bank Charges	490	490	490	490	490	490	490	490	490	490	490	490	5880
Cleaning	80	80	80	80	80	80	80	80	80	80	80	80	960

JIM'S CAR CARE CENTRE PROFIT AND LOSS PROJECTION (Cont'd)

	1999						2000						YEAR
	July	Aug	Sept	Oct	Nov	Dec	Jan	Feb	March	April	May	June	
Credit Card Charges	304	320	288	248	304	320	240	272	320	304	320	320	3560
Depreciation	980	980	980	980	980	980	980	980	980	980	980	980	11760
Donations	20	20	20	20	20	20	20	20	20	20	20	20	240
Entertainment	70	70	70	70	70	70	70	70	70	70	70	70	840
Freight & Cartage	304	320	288	248	304	320	240	272	320	304	320	320	3560
Hire of Pl. & Equip.	30	30	30	30	30	30	30	30	30	30	30	30	360
Insurance	0	0	1000	0	0	3400	0	0	0	0	0	0	4400
Interest	424	424	367	329	275	240	244	218	167	157	157	157	3159
Light & Power	0	800	0	0	800	0	0	800	0	0	800	0	3200
Motor Running	1660	1660	1660	1660	1660	1660	1660	1660	1660	1660	1660	1660	19920
Permits & Fees	60	60	60	60	60	60	60	60	60	60	60	60	720
Postage	80	80	80	80	80	80	80	80	80	80	80	80	960
Printing & Stationery	600	200	310	400	200	400	900	200	200	300	210	320	4240

JIM'S CAR CARE CENTRE PROFIT AND LOSS PROJECTION (Cont'd)

	1999						2000						YEAR
	July	Aug	Sept	Oct	Nov	Dec	Jan	Feb	March	April	May	June	
Registration Fees	400	0	0	0	300	0	0	0	400	0	0	0	1100
Rent	2400	2400	2400	2400	2400	2400	2400	2400	2400	2400	2400	2400	28800
Repairs & Maintenance	360	360	360	360	360	360	360	360	360	360	360	360	4320
Security	190	190	190	190	190	190	190	190	190	190	190	190	2280
Staff & Customer Amenities	456	480	432	372	456	480	360	408	480	456	480	480	5340
Subscriptions	80	80	80	80	80	80	80	80	80	80	80	80	960
Superannuation	1288	1288	1288	1288	1288	1288	1288	1288	1288	1288	1288	1288	15456
Telephone	600	600	600	600	600	600	600	600	600	600	600	600	7200
Tool Replacem't	60	60	60	60	60	60	60	60	60	60	60	60	720
Wages	18400	18400	18400	18400	18400	18400	18400	18400	18400	18400	18400	18400	220800
Workshop Supplies	274	288	259	223	274	288	216	245	288	274	288	288	3205
	33410	34280	33592	32468	33561	36096	32848	33063	32823	32443	33223	32533	400340
Net Profit	5350	6520	3128	-848	5199	4704	-2248	1617	7977	6317	7577	8267	53560

JIM'S CAR CARE CENTRE CASH FLOW PROJECTION

	1999						2000						
	Jul	Aug	Sep	Oct	Nov	Dec	Jan	Feb	Mar	Apr	May	Jun	YEAR
Opening Balance	-40000	-31857	-26483	-18595	-13701	-14578	-11029	-2616	-4128	-1254	7856	14286	-40000
Receipts													
Sales	80000	76000	80000	72000	62000	76000	80000	60000	68000	80000	76000	80000	890000
	40000	44143	53517	53405	48299	61422	68971	57384	63872	78746	83856	94286	850000
Payments													
Accountancy	400	1200	400	400	400	400	400	400	400	400	400	400	5600
Advertising	3400	3400	3400	3400	3400	3400	3400	3400	3400	3400	3400	3400	40800
Bank Charges	490	490	490	490	490	490	490	490	490	490	490	490	5880
Cleaning	80	80	80	80	80	80	80	80	80	80	80	80	960
Credit Card Charges	320	304	320	288	248	304	320	240	272	320	304	320	3560
Donations	20	20	20	20	20	20	20	20	20	20	20	20	240
Entertainment	70	70	70	70	70	70	70	70	70	70	70	70	840
Freight & Cartage	320	304	320	288	248	304	320	240	272	320	304	320	3560

JIM'S CAR CARE CENTRE CASH FLOW PROJECTION (Cont'd)

	1999		2000										YEAR
	Jul	Aug	Sep	Oct	Nov	Dec	Jan	Feb	Mar	Apr	May	Jun	
Hire of Pl. & Equip.	30	30	30	30	30	30	30	30	30	30	30	30	360
Insurance	0	0	1000	0	0	3400	0	0	0	0	0	0	4400
Interest	267	267	212	177	124	91	97	74	28	0	0	0	1336
Light & Power	0	800	0	0	800	0	0	800	0	0	800	0	3200
Loans	314	314	314	314	314	314	314	314	314	314	314	314	3768
Motor Running	1660	1660	1660	1660	1660	1660	1660	1660	1660	1660	1660	1660	19920
Permits & Fees	60	60	60	60	60	60	60	60	60	60	60	60	720
Postage	80	80	80	80	80	80	80	80	80	80	80	80	960
Printing & Stationery	600	200	310	400	200	400	900	200	200	300	210	320	4240
Purchases	39200	37240	39200	35280	30380	37240	39200	29400	33320	39200	37240	39200	436100
Registration Fees	400	0	0	0	300	0	0	0	400	0	0	0	1100
Rent	2400	2400	2400	2400	2400	2400	2400	2400	2400	2400	2400	2400	28800
Repairs & Maintenance	360	360	360	360	360	360	360	360	360	360	360	360	4320

JIM'S CAR CARE CENTRE CASH FLOW PROJECTION (Cont'd)

| | 1999 | | | | | | 2000 | | | | | | |
	Jul	Aug	Sep	Oct	Nov	Dec	Jan	Feb	Mar	Apr	May	Jun	YEAR
Security	190	190	190	190	190	190	190	190	190	190	190	190	2280
Staff & Customer Amenities	480	456	480	432	372	456	480	360	408	480	456	480	5340
Subscriptions	80	80	80	80	80	80	80	80	80	80	80	80	960
Superannuation	1288	1288	1288	1288	1288	1288	1288	1288	1288	1288	1288	1288	15456
Telephone	600	600	600	600	600	600	600	600	600	600	600	600	7200
Tool Replacem't	60	60	60	60	60	60	60	60	60	60	60	60	720
Wages	18400	18400	18400	18400	18400	18400	18400	18400	18400	18400	18400	18400	220800
Workshop Supplies	288	274	288	259	223	274	288	216	245	288	274	288	3204
	71857	70627	72112	67106	62877	72451	71587	61512	65127	70890	69570	70910	826624
Closing Balance	-31857	-26483	-18595	-13701	-14578	-11029	-2616	-4128	-1254	7856	14286	23376	23376

BALANCE SHEET PROJECTIONS

30 June	2000	2001	2002	2003	2004
Current Assets					
Cash on Hand	310	310	700	700	1,200
Cash at Bank	23,376	73,450	30,000	52,000	80,000
Inventory	29,640	29,640	60,000	60,000	90,000
Sundry Debtors	13,000	15,000	30,000	30,000	60,000
Other Current Assets	1,200	1,200	2,400	2,400	3,600
	67,526	119,600	123,100	145,100	234,800
Non-Current Assets					
Plant & Equipment	58,960	47,300	100,000	90,000	150,000
	126,486	166,900	223,100	235,100	384,800
Current Liabilities					
Creditors	54,133	52,000	60,000	90,000	140,000
Borrowings	3,768	3,768	12,000	12,000	12,000
	57,901	55,768	72,000	102,000	152,000
Non-Current Liabilities					
Borrowings	13,164	10,100	60,000	60,000	60,000
	71,065	65,868	132,000	162,000	212,000
Net Assets	55,421	101,032	91,100	73,100	172,800
Owners' Equity	$55,421	$101,032	$91,100	$73,100	$172,800

Funding

The business has relied upon funds provided by a bank overdraft and loans. Earnings have been withdrawn from the business so as to enable the owners to repay their personal debt. Although this policy has resulted in the proprietors owning their home, it has left the business highly geared and susceptible to a downturn. In the future there will be a need to retain profits in the business to enable it to fund its growth. A tight collection policy has been maintained to keep funds required for debtors to a minimum. This will need to continue. It is intended to fund expansion by borrowings and the leasing of equipment.

Because of the growth plans, it is essential that there be a close monitoring of performance against budgets to ensure that the equity position does not deteriorate.

Issues relating to increased levels of debtors and stock will need to be addressed as growth occurs.

Management

The owners recognise that the development of a structured management system is a critical element to the success of the business. This system needs to be designed and documented. It will include two key features:

1. A statement of procedures and standards for use by staff. This will be in the form of a manual which will reduce the dependence of the business on individuals.

2. A guide for the owners to ensure that the procedures are consistent with the future path of the business.

The system will cover the following areas:

➡ The organisational structure

➡ Employees

➠ Reporting

➠ Financial controls

➠ Sales

➠ Operations

➠ Budgeting.

In the first year those systems which already exist in the business will be refined and documented. This action will commence immediately and be continually refined. They will provide an operating system for the business and a management model which will be passed on to a general manager when he is appointed in the future. This way the business will be less dependent on the day-to-day control by the owners.

Marketing

The owners have identified the three key expectations of the customers as being:

1. Quality

2. Good service

3. Competitive pricing.

A marketing program will be developed to ensure these expectations are met. A strong system of quality control will be introduced to achieve this. The business is already positioned in its demographic area as a long-term participant; however, price is an issue in the marketplace. So as to reduce the significance of price it will be essential that a high quality of service be maintained and a unique selling point be identified. This unique selling point will be used to establish, then maintain, a sustainable competitive advantage. It will also assist in maximising the business's economic profit and increase its value.

The marketing efforts will result in the business being recognised as having and providing:

➠ A readily identifiable image;

➠ A high quality product and service.

SWOT Analysis

Strengths

● Essential products and services

● Perception in the marketplace as a specialist in the field

● Size of the marketplace

● Consistency in the manner in which customers are handled.

Weaknesses

● Reliance on the owners

● Strength of the competition

● Lack of finance and a limited resource base

● Immature business

● Lack of formalised systems

● Lack of financial understanding

● Staff motivation

● Lack of systems to measure staff performance.

Opportunities

● Ability to reach maturity within a relatively short time span.

● Creation of strategic alliances with other businesses in the area

- Market demand

- Possibility of franchising.

Threats

- The Asian economic downturn

- Backyard repairers

- Supply of competent tradespeople

- Growth beyond the systems and financial controls

- The likelihood of new competition.

The business will attempt to build on its strengths and promote its position as a specialist in the marketplace. Action will be taken to reduce, and where possible eliminate, the weaknesses. An ongoing process of review will be installed so as to enable the owners to consider opportunities as they arise and to develop strategies to capitalise on them. At the same time threats will be reviewed and actions taken so as to minimise their effect on the business.

THE ACTION PLAN FOR THE YEAR 1999-2000

No.	Action	Priority	Time for Completion	To be Done by	Resources Needed
1	Install a new computer system	Urgent	30 June 1999	Marney	Leasing finance
2	Set up customer focus group	Urgent	30 June 1999	James	In conjunction with staff
3	Meet w/ accountant to discuss findings from focus group	High	2 July 1999	James	In conjunction w/ accountant
4	Complete year's fin. statem'ts	High	21 July 1999	Accountant	In conjunction with Marney
5	Meet w/ accountant to review year end figures and discuss key performance indicators	High	31 July 1999	James	In conjunction with Marney
6	Prepare a thank-you letter to be sent to each customer after completing a job	Medium	31 Aug 1999	Marney	In conjunction with James
7	Install a suggestion box	Medium	30 Sept 1999	James	Tradesmen
8	Complete sales procedure manual	Medium	31 Dec 1999	Marney	In conjunction with marketing consultants
9	Review adequacy of key performance indicators	High	31 Jan 2000	Marney	In conjunction w/ accountant
10	Set benchmarks for 2001	Medium	31 Mar 2000	Marney	In conjunction w/ accountant
11	Review the objectives	High	31 May 2000	Marn. & Jim	In conjunction w/ accountant
12	Prepare action plan for 2001	High	31 May 2000	Marney	In conjunction w/ accountant

---

KEY POINTS

☛ You don't need to write a wordy thesis on your plans for the future.

☛ The planning period should not be too short, nor should it be too long.

☛ The details become more general as you progress in the plan. That is, the plan should be detailed for the first year and general by the last year.

☛ The plan should be a working document, not an academic exercise.

✳ ✳ ✳ ✳ ✳

If your plan is being prepared for your internal management use, and this is the main reason why you should plan, then there is no need to have it professionally written. If your plan is being written to raise finance (then I would contend that it is a loan application rather than a plan), some consideration should be given as to whether outside help is required to ensure that it is adequately presented. If you engage professional help, make sure that the plan is written in your language, language that you understand. After all, the plan is your work. If it isn't, then it is unlikely that you will use it as you should.

You should not obtain a copy of another plan and adapt it to your business. Each business is different, each business has different goals. For that reason, I view the available business planning software programs that are on the market with a degree of scepticism. An effective business plan cannot be written by filling in templates.

It may be that simply collating the worksheets you have prepared as you have gone through the steps discussed in this book and binding them as a document is all that you need to do. Together, they are your plan. The one document that really matters is your action plan. This is the real business plan. You can formalise it if you want, and that may be useful, but it may not be necessary.

The traditional way of preparing a business plan is to write an essay in the following format (or in a similar fashion):

- A cover sheet showing your business name and the date
- A list of contents
- An executive summary
- The management
- The business history
- The market and the competition
- A market plan
- An operations plan
- Financial forecasts
- Financial requirements
- Historical financial data.

Is all this really necessary? When you consider that a high proportion of business plans sit gathering dust in the bottom of filing cabinets and drawers, the answer would probably be no. As contended earlier, all this is not even necessary when giving the plan to your financier. Remember, when it comes to the crunch, he is in the business of selling money to you. If he is satisfied that you fulfil his lending criteria he will give you the funds, business plan or not.

I would rather see an effective plan compiled and followed through, one that is practical and referred to often. One where the main input has come from yourself. One that is yours because you have written it. You may have needed outside help along the way. But the plan should be yours and yours to use. Anything less will most likely end up in the rubbish bin. If the exercise results in an action plan that is realistic, in line with your objectives, implemented and monitored, then that is far more valuable than the traditionally-written business plan.

12

MEASURING PERFORMANCE AND REVISING THE PLAN

IT IS NECESSARY for you to monitor your action plan, compare your budgets to actual performance and investigate any variances. If you don't, there is no way you can measure the progress of your business towards the objectives you have set out in your plan. It is impossible for you to predict all the changes that may affect your business. New opportunities and threats will arise – both externally (driven by government policy, your competitors and suppliers) and from within your business – which you need to recognise promptly. You will need to adjust quickly so that your business remains on the path you have laid down for it.

Your business plan is designed to help you achieve specific objectives. Although these may be less definable three, four and five years out, your plan is a reflection of your vision as to where you want your business to be in the future. Variances from your budgeted performance must therefore be analysed so as to alert you to:

➠ Changes in your operations, and their effect on your results

➠ The need to revise budgets

➠ The actions you must take to bring the business back into line with your objectives.

You should prepare a copy of your budgets but, in the copy, divide the monthly columns into two. The first column contains your budgeted figures, the second contains your actual results. You may decide to add another column into which you enter the variance.

An example is shown below in respect of a summarised profit and loss budget. By removing the detail it is easy to focus on the important figures which are the sales, gross profit, expenses and the net result. The reasons for the variances can be discovered by investigating the detailed figures.

PROFIT AND LOSS BUDGET

	Budget	Actual	Variance
Sales	15,000	16,000	1,000
Gross Profit	6,000	5,600	(400)
Expenses	4,500	4,800	(300)
Net Profit	1,500	800	(700)

It is essential that you analyse the reasons for the variances. Just to say that sales exceeded budget by $1,000, gross profit was down by $400, expenses were $300 more than expected, resulting in $700 less net profit than budgeted is not enough. You need to ask why sales were up by $1,000, why gross profit was down, expenses were up and net profit was less than anticipated.

In this case it may be that you received a large order which you discounted, resulting in a lower gross margin. Additional delivery costs may have been incurred in filling the order, explaining the increased expenditure. As the answers emerge you will gain a deeper understanding of your business. This will help you to make better management decisions and result in an improvement in the performance of your business. It may be that the assumptions you made when you prepared your budgets were incorrect. By identifying this, you can adjust your budgets and therefore improve your forecasting as time goes on.

You should probably monitor your key performance indicators at least weekly. If you don't, you will be letting the business run you. Business management is about planning and control, and this requires you to regularly record your results for analysis. Don't let yourself fall into the trap of thinking it is too much trouble.

You may have identified as a key performance indicator the number of people entering your store. How do you measure this? Completion of the table below on a daily basis will help.

Date:

Time	People in Shop	Staff at Work	Total Sales
9 – 10	....	....	....
10 – 11	....	....	....
11 – 12	....	....	....
12 – 1	....	....	....
1 – 2	....	....	....
2 – 3	....	....	....
3 – 4	....	....	....
4 – 5	....	....	....
DAY			

The importance of regular review cannot be over-emphasised. This holds for the overall plan as well. You goals can change and if they do, your plan should be modified to reflect those goals. The plan should not be a rigid, inflexible document. It should be an adaptable management tool that serves as the road map to help you achieve the vision you have for your business.

13

PREPARING A PLAN FOR A NEW BUSINESS

BEFORE YOU start up a small business you need to ensure it is viable. This requires the preparation of a feasibility study; that is, you need to evaluate your business idea. This is the first step in developing a business plan for a new business. There is little point in going further if the proposal does not stack up.

But before that you need to ask yourself:

? Will I find the business enjoyable?

? Will it be stimulating?

? Do I believe in the products or services it will be selling?

? Do I have the necessary experience and qualifications to operate it successfully?

? What are my personal goals and does the business proposal fit in with them?

If you answer 'no' to these questions, stop right there. Business success rarely comes easily and would be unlikely if these criteria are not met.

Now you need to describe your business idea. Write a summary listing:

➠ What the business will do

➠ What products you will offer

➠ Where you want the business to be in one, two and three years' time.

Consider the table below. This is extracted from information in a publication titled *Starting and Managing a Small Business of Your Own* (Small Business Administration, Washington DC, US Government Printing Office, 1981). Although the information relates to the situation in the USA, and is dated, it would be reasonable to assume that similar requirements prevail in Australia. If your proposal includes one of the kinds of businesses in the table, reference to it should help you decide if there is room for you in the marketplace.

NUMBER OF INHABITANTS PER STORE BY SELECTED KIND OF BUSINESS – NATIONAL AVERAGE

Kind of Business	No. of Inhabitants per Store
Food Stores	
Candy, nut & confectionery stores	31,409
Dairy products stores	41,587
Grocery stores	1,534
Meat and fish (seafood) markets	17,876
Retail bakeries	12,563
Eating, Drinking Places	
Cafeterias	19,341

Kind of Business	No. of Inhabitants per Store
Drinking places (alcoholic beverages)	2,414
Refreshment places	3,622
Restaurants, lunchrooms, caterers	1,583
General Merchandise	
General merchandise stores	9,837
Variety stores	10,373
Apparel & Accessory Stores	
Family clothing stores	16,890
Men's & boys' clothing & furnishing stores	11,832
Shoe stores	9,350
Women's accessory & specialty stores	25,824
Women's ready to wear stores	7,012
Building Material, Hardware & Farm Equipment Dealers	
Farm equipment dealers	14,793
Hardware stores	10,206
Paint, glass & wallpaper stores	22,454
Timber & other building materials dealers	8,124
Automotive Dealers	
Boat dealers	61,526
Gasoline service stations	1,195
Household trailer dealers	44,746
Motor vehicle dealers – new & used cars	6,000
Motor vehicle dealers – used cars only	17,160
Tyre, battery & accessory dealers	8,764

Kind of Business	No. of Inhabitants per Store
Miscellaneous	
Antique & second-hand stores	17,169
Book & stationery stores	28,584
Florists	13,531
Fuel oil dealers	25,425
Garden supply stores	65,118
Gift, novelty & souvenir shops	26,313
Hay, grain & feed stores	16,978
Hobby, toy & game stores	61,340
Jewellery stores	13,495
Liquefied petroleum gas (bottled gas) dealers	32,803
Liquor stores	6,359
Mail order houses	44,559
Merchandising machine operators	44,067
Optical goods stores	62,878
Pharmacies	4,268
Sporting goods stores	27,063
Furniture, Home Furnishings & Equipment	
Drapery, curtain & upholstery stores	62,460
Floor covering stores	29,543
Furniture stores	7,210
Household appliance stores	12,585
Musical instrument stores	46,332
Radio & television stores	20,346
Record shops	112,144

Make a list of any barriers to commencing the business, such as qualification restrictions, licensing requirements and financing needs.

Then ask yourself if the time is right to enter the business. This requires a consideration of the prevailing economic conditions.

Economic performance indicators reflect the state of the economy. These can be obtained from the Australian Bureau of Statistics and include:

➼ Average weekly earnings

➼ Balance of trade

➼ Consumer Price Index (CPI)

➼ Gross National Product (GNP)

➼ Household expenditure

➼ New car registrations

➼ New housing starts

➼ Retail sales

➼ Unemployment rate.

Extract the statistics for the past five years and enter the figures as at 30 June each year into the table opposite. Enter an arrow pointing up, down or sideways in the appropriate row to indicate whether the indicator is increasing, decreasing, or moving sideways.

This will enable you to identify the trends. When you have done this you need to ask:

? Are average weekly earnings growing?

? Is the balance of trade increasing or decreasing?

? Is inflation growing, stagnating or is there deflation?

? Is GNP growing or contracting or is there no growth?

? What is happening with the level of consumer spending? This can be measured by the indicators for household expenditure, new car registrations, new housing starts and retail sales and is a measure of demand which influences business activity.

? Is the unemployment rate rising or falling?

? Are interest rates high or low?

Indicator	1995	1996	1997	1998	1999	Trend
Average Weekly Earnings	......	......	......	......	......	......
Balance of Trade	......	......	......	......	......	......
Consumer Price Index	......	......	......	......	......	......
Gross National Product	......	......	......	......	......	......
Household Expenditure	......	......	......	......	......	......
New Car Registrations	......	......	......	......	......	......
New Housing Starts	......	......	......	......	......	......
Retail Sales	......	......	......	......	......	......
Unemployment Rate	......	......	......	......	......	......
90-Day Bank Bill Rate	......	......	......	......	......	......
Ten-Year Bond Rate	......	......	......	......	......	......

This exercise should be done with regard to the state of the economy at the time of evaluating the proposal – that is, how do the previous two years compare? How do the previous two quarters compare? When you have finished it you will have an idea as to whether the time is right to undertake your business proposal.

The economy operates in cycles and all industry sectors will not be at the same stage of the cycle at the same time. They vary in length and, despite some opinions to the contrary, no one can predict when the current phase of the business cycle will change. However, the indicators can tell us where we are in the cycle. Consumer confidence figures may suggest where the economy is heading, but these are just opinions and should not be relied upon when the economic indicators indicate otherwise. It may be that the economy is in the wrong phase to consider commencing a business proposal. Awareness of this may help prevent you make a major mistake.

WILL THE PROPOSAL PROVIDE A POSITIVE ECONOMIC PROFIT?

If you are satisfied that the time is right, you then need to investigate the proposal. Will the business proposition provide you with an acceptable living standard and increase your wealth? That is, as was discussed in Chapter 6, Economic Value Added, will there be an economic profit? If not, the proposal should be abandoned. You should therefore calculate the EVA for the proposal. Before you can do this, though, you need to prepare the financial budgets. These are discussed in Chapter 9.

The Australian Tax Office has recently developed some financial benchmarks for specific cash industries. These may be useful when considering whether the returns you are hoping to achieve from your business venture are realistic. They are shown below.

PRELIMINARY FINANCIAL RATIOS FOR SOME CASH INDUSTRIES

	Gross Profit (%)	Net Profit (%)	Wages/ Turnover (%)
Building Industry			
Bricklaying	80-85	40-45	10-15
Carpentry	65-75	35-40	15-20

	Gross Profit (%)	Net Profit (%)	Wages/ Turnover (%)
House construction	55-60	18-20	10-15
Painting	75-80	35-40	20-25
Plumbing	60-65	20-25	15-20
Roofing	65-70	25-30	15-20

Fruit & Vegetable Growing & Wholesale

	Gross Profit (%)	Net Profit (%)	Wages/ Turnover (%)
Apple & pear growers	85-90	20-25	20-25
Grape growers	85-90	30-35	20-25
Fruit & vegetable wholesalers & retailers	25-30	5-10	10-15
Vegetable growers	85-90	20-25	15-20

Clothing Manufacture & Wholesale

	Gross Profit (%)	Net Profit (%)	Wages/ Turnover (%)
Clothing manufacture	65-70	20-25	20-25
Clothing wholesale	40-45	10-15	10-15

Hospitality

	Gross Profit (%)	Net Profit (%)	Wages/ Turnover (%)
Licensed clubs	70-75	8-10	20-25
Pubs, taverns & bars	50-55	8-10	10-15
Restaurants & cafes	60-65	10-15	20-30

Road Transport

	Gross Profit (%)	Net Profit (%)	Wages/ Turnover (%)
Couriers		45-55	15-20
Road freight		25-35	15-20

Taxi Industry

	Gross Profit (%)	Net Profit (%)	Wages/ Turnover (%)
Taking per total km travelled	69¢		

To help you further, the Small Business Industry Performance Ratios in Australia for 1993/94 from *Small Business in Australia 1995* (ABS Catalogue No. 1321.0) are set out below.

Industry	Profit Margin (%)	Return on Assets (%)	Return on Net Worth (%)	Long-Term Debt to Equity
Manufacturing	8.5	15.2	48.4	0.9
Construction	5.5	10.7	62.7	1.4
Wholesale Trade	3.4	7.8	35.4	1.0
Retail Trade	4.4	12.9	38.0	0.9
Accommodation Cafes & Restaurants	5.5	4.9	9.9	0.5
Transport & Storage	5.4	7.5	32.3	1.5
Finance & Insurance	29.2	3.3	9.4	0.7
Property & Business Services	15.6	9.3	25.7	0.9
Private Community Services	19.1	27.0	81.7	1.0
Cultural & Recreational Services	6.5	8.5	23.8	0.9
Personal & Other Services	8.0	6.9	11.6	0.4

Source: *Small Business in Australia 1995*, Australian Bureau of Statistics Catalogue No. 1321.0

The ratios were calculated as follows:

$$Profit\ Margin = \frac{Operating\ Profit\ Before\ Tax}{Operating\ Income} \times 100$$

$$Return\ on\ Assets = \frac{Operating\ Profit\ Before\ Tax}{Total\ Assets} \times 100$$

$$Return\ on\ Net\ Worth = \frac{Operating\ Profit\ Before\ Tax}{Net\ Worth} \times 100$$

$$Long\text{-}Term\ Debt\ to\ Equity = \frac{Non\text{-}Current\ Liabilities}{Net\ Worth}$$

SETTING YOUR TARGET PROFIT

Whilst the benchmarks are an invaluable tool, their weakness is that they are based on averages, and averages can be distorted by extreme results either on the high or low side. For this reason you should develop a model for your own business. The profitability model below is based on a model which is part of the *Business Development for Results* manual from Results Practice Consulting Pty Ltd.

Your business is an investment, and when we invest we expect a return on our money. That return is affected by the risk that we perceive is applicable to the particular investment. The chapter on economic value added and the earlier comments have hopefully convinced you that you should be concerned with an economic return. That is, a return for the investment, which includes your input into your business and the capital you have invested. Whilst not mentioned in their manual, the Results Practice Consulting model encompasses this.

The return from your business should, therefore, reflect three components. These are:

1. A return for the time you spend in your business

2. A return for the money you have invested in your business

3. A return for the risk of being in business.

	$
Reasonable owners' remuneration	Calculate the amount you would be paid, if you were an employee, for the hours you work in your business. ....
Return on investment	Calculate the return you could expect from your money if you invested it elsewhere. ....
Profit	Calculate the return you require to compensate you for the risk of being in business. ....
TARGET PROFIT	

Again, reference to Chapter 6 on EVA will help you decide on the appropriate returns you require when you undertake this exercise.

KNOWING YOUR BREAK-EVEN POINT

It is essential that you know how much you need to sell to break even – that is, the level of sales where there is neither a profit or a loss.

Costs can be broken up into two categories:

1. Fixed costs – costs incurred no matter what the turnover (e.g. rent); and

2. Variable costs – costs that change in relation to the turnover (e.g. purchases).

A business with no sales will have a loss equivalent to its fixed costs. Identification of the fixed and variable costs will enable you to calculate your break-even point.

The break-even point is calculated as follows:

$$Break\text{-}even\ point\ =\ \frac{Fixed\ Costs}{Contribution\ Margin}$$

The contribution margin is calculated as:

$$Contribution\ margin\ =\ \frac{Sales\ -\ Variable\ Costs}{Sales}$$

EXAMPLE

Let us assume the financial statements of the business you are considering disclose:

Sales	$200,000
Variable costs	$140,000
Fixed costs	$20,000

$$Contribution\ margin\ =\ \frac{200,000\ -\ 140,000}{200,000}$$

$$=\ 30\%$$

$$Break\text{-}even\ point\ =\ \frac{20,000}{0.30}$$

$$=\ \$66,666$$

In this example sales of $66,666 will be necessary for the business to break even.

After fixed costs have been covered by the contribution margin, the contribution margin becomes the rate at which increased sales contribute to profit. An understanding of these concepts is essential to your pricing policies and your planning.

ESTIMATING YOUR LIVING EXPENSES

The business, if it is to be your full-time occupation, will have to provide you with a living. You need to know what your living expenses are so that you can ensure the business will be able to support your lifestyle. If it can't, you will need to consider whether you are prepared to change your living habits. Sufficient profit and cash will need to be provided to support your personal needs, as well as meeting your business and taxation commitments. An example of an estimation of monthly expenses follows:

	$
Food	280
Clothing	120
Mortgage Repayments	540
Rates	100
Telephone	40
Electricity	60
Motor running	300
Entertainment	60
Education	100
Insurances	120
Other Living Expenses	60
	$1,780

In this example the business will need to provide you with an after-tax income of at least $21,360 per annum for you to maintain your current lifestyle.

CAN YOU FINANCE THE PROPOSAL?

Assuming the proposal holds up, you next need to establish whether you have the means to finance the project. This involves a consideration of your personal financial position, your commitments and your capacity to borrow. You need to draw up a statement of assets and liabilities. An example is shown below.

Statement of Assets and Liabilities as at 31 Jan 1998

Assets	
Home	250,000
Cash at Bank	12,000
Investments	140,000
Car	15,000
Personal Effects	40,000
	457,000
Liabilities	
Credit Cards	1,000
Mortgage	15,000
	16,000
Net Worth	**$441,000**

In this example, it is clear that although you do not have a lot of cash available, you have a sizeable equity in your home which can be used as security for a business loan, and investments which may be realised to provide further funds.

HOW MUCH WILL YOU NEED?

You now need to look at the funding requirements of the business.

These can be broken up into three components:

1. The costs of investigating the proposal
2. The costs of setting up the business
3. The cost of providing sufficient working capital to run the business.

Costs of Investigating the Proposal

These costs could include:

➠ Travel and accommodation

➠ Telephone calls, faxes, stationery

➠ Market research

➠ Accountancy costs for the review, analysis, and preparation of budgets

➠ Legal costs if a solicitor is used to investigate the legality of the business operations.

Costs of Setting up the Business

These could include:

➠ The cost of plant and equipment needed

➠ The cost of establishing your trading structure

➠ Borrowing costs for the loan to finance the business.

Initial Costs and Working Capital to Run the Business

Such costs may be, for example:

➠ Legal costs for preparation and review of the lease

➠ Rent in advance

➠ Bank account and merchant facility establishment costs

➡ Sufficient capital to meet the initial overheads

➡ Stock

➡ Stationery

➡ Licences, permits and registrations

➡ Insurance premiums.

EXAMPLE

Costs of Investigating the Proposal

Accountancy	1,000
Legal Costs	500
Other	500
	2,000
Costs of Purchasing Equipment	80,000
Legal Costs re: Structure	1,200
	81,200

Initial Costs and Working Capital

Borrowing Costs	2,200
Lease Preparation and Review	1,800
Rent in Advance	2,400
Working Capital	24,000
Insurance	3,400
	33,800
Funds Required	$117,000
Personal Funds Available	12,000
Required Borrowing	$105,000

SOURCES OF FINANCE

Now you need to consider where you are going to borrow the money from. Short-term finance should be used to fund the short-term needs of a business. There is an old adage that says you shouldn't borrow short to finance long. This means that short-term borrowings should not be used to finance long-term assets. For example, it would be unwise to finance the acquisition of business premises on a 90-day commercial bill facility. Even though the bill may be rolled over every 90 days, there is a chance that the facility might not be renewed. If alternative finance could not be arranged, you might be forced to sell the premises at a less than favourable price. To reiterate, long-term finance should be used to fund the long-term business needs.

The items making up the plant and equipment of a business are medium to long-term assets. The type of finance used should be related to the asset's expected life. No one wants to be paying for equipment long after it is gone. Commercial hire purchase, personal loans, and leasing may be appropriate forms of finance for this class of asset.

Type Of Cost	Source of Finance
Costs of Investigating the Business	Your Own Funds
Plant and Equipment	Your Own Funds
	Bank Loans
	Personal Loans
	Commercial Hire Purchase
	Leases
Stock and Debtors	Your Own Funds
	Factoring
	Bank Loans

Type Of Cost	Source of Finance
Working capital requirements	Your Own Funds
	Bank Loans
	Bank Overdraft

Your Own Funds

You cannot expect to commence a business without putting your capital at risk. Why would a lender lend to you if you were not prepared to risk your own funds? It is prudent to have facilities in place to finance two months' worth of operating expenses. This provides a safety buffer should business slow down.

Bank Overdrafts

An overdraft is the most flexible source of borrowing available. It is an arrangement with a bank that enables you to draw funds on a cheque account up to a predetermined limit. Funds are only drawn when needed and interest is charged on the daily balance. Overdrafts carry with them establishment fees and periodic service fees. They are repayable at call and are most effectively used to finance short-term working capital requirements. Overdraft interest rates are normally higher than long-term rates.

Bank Loans

The bank can provide various types of loans to finance the business. It may be possible to arrange a housing loan to provide the funding, if you have sufficient equity in your home. However, more than likely a term loan will be offered. A term loan is a loan normally for a period of between two and ten years. The facility is fully drawn down and repayments of principal and interest are made in regular instalments. They are not an appropriate form of short-term finance, but more suited to longer-term financing and appropriate for the financing of the acquisition of plant and equipment. Interest rates may be either variable or fixed and are usually charged on the daily balance.

Personal Loans

Although personal loans are normally used to finance consumer goods, they can be used to finance business needs. Interest rates are higher for personal loans than for term loans, as they are unsecured. A personal loan may be appropriate for the financing of plant and equipment.

Commercial Hire Purchase

Commercial hire purchase is sometimes referred to as a lease purchase. The lender buys the asset and hires it to you for an agreed period. At the end of the period you own the equipment. There may be a balloon payment at the end of the term (if the repayments are not sufficient to extinguish the debt).

Leases

A lease is not a loan. The person owning the goods agrees to lease the goods to you for a fixed period of time for a fixed rental, with an option for you to purchase the goods at a predetermined value (the residual). Leasing may be an appropriate form of finance for plant and equipment and motor vehicles.

Factoring

At the risk of offending those who see it as an answer to funding a rapidly-growing business, I have always viewed factoring as an expensive finance of last resort. Factoring involves selling your debtors to a financier who advances a percentage of the monies owed to you (often 80%). The balance is paid (less a fee) when the debt is collected. This frees up the cash you would otherwise have tied up in debtors from your credit sales. Once entered into, this can be a difficult form of financing to get out of.

TYPES OF LENDERS

The main types of financiers are:

- Banks
- Building societies
- Credit unions
- Finance companies.

PREPARING THE PLAN

At this stage you probably will have enough information to approach your bank for a loan. A brief description of the business proposal, accompanied by your statement of asset and liabilities, the feasibility study and the budgeted projections will be enough for your bank manager to make a decision. He will in fact say you have a business plan. But it will not be enough for you. Business can be fun, but it is not a game. It carries with it the risk of loss of your hard-earned capital. For this reason you need to go further.

Completion of the following questionnaires will result in a thorough assessment of the issues you will need to consider. The areas which need addressing will form part of your action plan. You don't need to waste time writing an essay about them. Simply answer them in the space provided and then prepare a list of things to do and the time you need to do them to overcome any problems they reveal. Including both the questionnaires and the action plan with the submission to your financier will show him you have analysed your proposition. However, the task should be done for *you*, not him.

Note: if there isn't sufficient space to write your answer, put down a number, number a sheet of paper and answer the question on that. Then staple the paper to the back of the questionnaire.

LOCATION QUESTIONNAIRE

The Location

Does it offer good exposure to customers? ....

Is it accessible? ....

Is there adequate parking? ....

Does it fulfil council regulations? ....

Are suppliers, banks and labour sources
nearby? ....

How long was the previous tenant there? ....

Are the surrounding businesses compatible
with yours? ....

Are the businesses in the area well
diversified? ....

Is there room for expansion? ....

Is there any likelihood of changes in the
area that might affect the business? ....

The Area

What is the population of the area you
will serve? ....

What percentage of the population can
you hope to serve? ....

Is the area growing or in decline? ....

Are most of homes in the area rented
or owned? ....

Are the area's residents the type of people
who will buy your products or services? ....

What is the average age of the residents? ....

What is the ethnic background of the
residents? ....

What is the occupation grouping of the
residents? ....

What is the income level of the residents? ....

The Premises

What floor space and dimensions do
you require? ....

Are the premises fitted out for your
requirements? ....

Are the premises well presented? ....

Are the premises secure? ....

Will the premises meet your future needs? ....

Will you need to spend money outfitting
the premises? ....

The Lease

Is there a lease? ....

How long will the lease run? ....

What are the lease costs? ....

Is the lease transferable? ....

Does the lease grant a right of assignment? ....

Does the lease impose any restrictions on
business activity? ....

Is the rent based on turnover or profits? ....

CUSTOMERS QUESTIONNAIRE

Who will your likely customer be?   ....

How old will he be?   ....

Where will he live?   ....

What will be his income level?   ....

How educated will he be?   ....

Will your customers be able to afford
your products?   ....

How many customers are you likely
to attract?   ....

Are there enough potential customers?   ....

Why will your customer choose to buy
from you?   ....

Is your customer price sensitive?   ....

What does your customer want from you?   ....

Why will he buy from you?   ....

How much will your customer buy
from you?   ....

How much will your customer spend
with you?   ....

How often will your customer buy
from you?   ....

When will your customers buy from you?   ....

Are your customers easily reached?   ....

PRODUCT QUESTIONNAIRE

How do the products compare to others? ....

Are the products in danger of becoming
out of fashion or obsolete? ....

Are the products fast or slow-moving? ....

At what stage are the products in their
lifestyles? ....

How well are the products presented? ....

How available are the products? ....

Do the products have a good reputation? ....

Are the products necessary or discretionary? ....

Who buys the products? ....

Do the products satisfy the needs of your
customers? ....

What influences the customers to buy
the products? ....

Do the products provide an acceptable
profit margin? ....

SUPPLIERS QUESTIONNAIRE

How many suppliers are there? ....

Are the suppliers reliable? ....

Will they offer satisfactory trading terms? ....

Will they be prepared to deal with you? ....

Are they able to supply a quality product?   ....

Will you be dependent on any one supplier?   ....

Are the suppliers conveniently located?   ....

Are the suppliers financially stable?   ....

COMPETITORS QUESTIONNAIRE

Who are your competitors?   ....

Where are your competitors located?   ....

How many competitors are there?   ....

How long have your competitors been there?   ....

How do your competitors' services compare to yours?   ....

What don't they offer their customers?   ....

Are there any known future competitors?   ....

What will differentiate you from the competition?   ....

What customer demands don't they satisfy?   ....

Are your competitors successful?   ....

Will the market support another participant?   ....

EMPLOYEE QUESTIONNAIRE

What jobs need to be done in the business?   ....

How much time will the jobs take?   ....

How many employees are needed to do them? ....

What skills do they need? ....

How should employees be recruited? ....

How should they be selected? ....

How should they be compensated? ....

How should they be motivated? ....

How should they be trained? ....

How should they be evaluated? ....

How should they be terminated? ....

Attach a job analysis to this questionnaire. There should be an analysis for each job. This should consist of a job description and a job specification. The job description should describe the nature, the requirements and the responsibilities of the job. The job specification should include the education level, experience, knowledge, and abilities required to perform the tasks outlined in the job description.

The two parts of a sample job analysis are presented below.

Job Description

Job Title: ....

General Description of Duties: ....

Major Duties: ....

Minor Duties: ....

Responsible to: ....

Job Specification

Job Title: ....

Education Level: ....

Experience Required: ....

Knowledge Required: ....

Abilities Required: ....

MARKETING QUESTIONNAIRE

What is your target market?   ....

How do you intend to reach that market?   ....

How are you going to promote your products? ....

How are you going to price your products?   ....

How are you going to distribute your products? ....

ORGANISATION QUESTIONNAIRE

What legal structure are you going to use?   ....

Have you drawn an organisational chart?   ....

Who is your accountant?   ....

Who is your banker?   ....

Who is your consultant?   ....

Who is your insurance broker?   ....

Who is your solicitor?   ....

RECORD-KEEPING QUESTIONNAIRE

Are you aware of the records you are required
to keep? ....

Are you aware of the records you should keep? ....

Have you discussed your record-keeping
requirements with your accountant? ....

Are you going to computerise? ....

Do you need to computerise? ....

Have you listed the reports you need to
produce? ....

Have you considered how often you need
to see the reports? ....

Have you identified your key performance
indicators? ....

Will your system report on your key
performance indicators? ....

THE PRELIMINARY ACTION PLAN FOR A NEW BUSINESS

There are things that must be done before you commence trading.
These are part of your business plan. As discussed previously, a
business plan without an action plan is not a plan at all. An example
of a preliminary action plan for a start-up business is shown below.

Action	When to be Done	When Done
Consider your suitability for the business	....	
Consider whether you can fund a business	....	

199

Action	When to be Done	When Done
Undertake a feasibility study	....	
Complete the business plan questionnaires	....	
Select a business name	....	
Select your accountant	....	
Select your banker	....	
Select your computer consultant	....	
Select your insurance broker	....	
Select your solicitor	....	
Set up the business's legal structure	....	
Open your bank account	....	
Obtain your finance	....	
Select your business premises	....	
Negotiate the rent and lease	....	
Obtain the necessary licences and permits	....	
Enter into the lease	....	
Connect the electricity, gas and water	....	
Prepare and fit out the premises	....	
Attend to your signage	....	
Have the telephone put on	....	

Action	When to be Done	When Done
Plan the stock layout	....	
Order the initial stock	....	
Arrange the insurances	....	
Design your business stationery	....	
Set up your record-keeping system	....	
Apply for your income Tax File Number	....	
Hire your staff	....	
Register as a group employer	....	
Arrange your workers' compensation insurance	....	
Arrange your initial promotions and advertising	....	
Open your doors	....	

CONCLUSION

BUSINESS PLANNING, like management, is an art. It is not an exact science. It requires a structured approach to help you outline the map for your business future. By forcing you to think about your goals and produce forecasts against which you can measure the performance of your business, it results in the identification of key performance indicators which you can manage. As a result, and by viewing it as an ongoing process (an integral part of management) which requires a regular review, business planning can lead to an increase in your wealth and the achievement of your goals.

ADVANTAGES OF PLANNING

A business plan, as we have seen, is useful for many reasons. For example, business planning:

➠ Helps you establish a road map for the future of your business

➠ Forces you to think about where your business is heading and whether that is in tune with your personal and business goals

➠ Provides a means of establishing indicators that you can use in controlling and managing the business

➠ Results in an improved understanding of how the business works

➠ Forces you to analyse your business

➠ Helps you identify problems the business is facing and forces you to consider means of overcoming them

➠ Assists you in adapting to market changes

➠ Helps you identify the strengths of your business and think of ways to utilise them to your benefit

➠ Helps you balance your growth and creates an awareness of the funding requirements for operations

➠ Forces you to become results-oriented by establishing and monitoring performance against targets

➠ Provides information for a lender and enables him or her to consider the likelihood of your future success

➠ Provides a tool to help achieve the real goal for your business, that is an increase in your net worth.

THE EXCUSES FOR NOT PLANNING

A number of excuses can be offered for not planning. For me, these are not valid – they are a result of misunderstanding the benefits that can be provided by taking the time to plan and then using the plan as an ongoing management tool. Some of these excuses are:

➠ Business plans are of little use

➠ I don't know where to start

➠ I am too busy

➠ They cost too much (my counter-argument: only if you use an external consultant to write the whole plan)

➠ I am successful, therefore I don't need to plan (to counter this, consider how much more successful you might be if you did plan).

Hopefully the contents of this book will have gone some way to refuting these arguments.

As a small business owner you have limited resources. You cannot utilise the specialised and often complex and costly planning methods used by large firms. However, you have one big advantage. You can be flexible and therefore can adapt more quickly to changes in the marketplace. You make the decisions and are not constrained by bureaucracy. But you need to have procedures in place that enable you to identify problems as they emerge. That is, you need to take an active approach to the opportunities and challenges faced by your firm. This involves an ongoing process of planning and review – in short, a business plan.

BIBLIOGRAPHY

The 24 Hour Business Plan
Ron Johnson, Century Ltd, Random House, 1990.

The Accountants' Boot Camp Session Notes
The Results Corporation, 4-7 June 1992.

The Australian Small Business Guide
Sara Williams and Bob Sims, Penguin Books, 1993.

Benchmarking Australia
Joanna MacNeil, Jonathon Testi, John Cupples, Malcolm Rimmer, Longman Business & Professional, 1993.

Benchmarking Workbook
Bengt Karlof, John Wiley & Sons, 1995.

Business Development for Results
Results Practice Consulting Pty Ltd, 1995.

Business Planning for Small Manufacturers
National Industry Extension Service, Australian Government Publishing Service, 1980.

Business Process Design and Performance Measurement
Results Accountants' Systems, 1998.

Cash Flow Management
National Industry Extension Service, Australian Government Publishing Service, 1982.

Control Records: The Key to Improving Retailing Profits
Department of Industry, Technology and Commerce Service, Australian Government Publishing Service, 1985.

Financial Budgeting in Small Business
Department of Industry, Technology and Commerce Service, Australian Government Publishing Service, 1985.

Financial Budgeting for Small Manufacturers
National Industry Extension Service, Australian Government Publishing Service, 1980.

How to Organise and Operate a Small Business in Australia
John W. English, Allen & Unwin, 1995.

How to Prepare a Business Plan
Edward Blackwell, Wrightbooks, 1992.

Making Small Business Work for You
Ian Birt, Rigby Heinemann, 1994.

Preparing a Business Plan
Matthew Record, How to Books Ltd, 1997.

Preparing and Implementing a Business Plan
Peter Haslock, Institute of Chartered Accountants, March 1999.

The Quest for Value
G. Bennett Stewart III, Harper Collins, 1991.

Small Business Financial Management in Australia
John W. English, Allen & Unwin, 1990.

Small Business Victoria Information Sheets

Starting Your New Business
Charles L. Martin, Crisp Publications Inc., 1988.

What You Can Do to Improve the Profitability of Your Business
Results Accountants' Systems Australasia Pty Ltd.

Your Own Business: A Practical Guide to Success
Wal Reynolds, Warwick Savage, Alan Williams, Thomas Nelson Australia, 1989.

INDEX

Property promoters create the illusion that negative gearing is a magic potion that will solve an investor's taxation problems. That is not necessarily so. This book takes an unbiased and objective look at the tax effect of a loss from a rental property. Our taxation system is involved, complex and unwieldy – so Tony Compton makes a point of providing practical advice in an easily read manner. Subjects include the purchase, tax return and the sale. This is a must read for any owner of, or anyone considering purchasing, a rental property.

For an investor, the cost of acquiring a parcel of shares is a capital cost and the shares become an asset. For a share trader, this cost is the cost of acquiring trading stock and is therefore an expense incurred in producing assessable income. The difference in the tax treatment between assets and stock – and between investors and traders – is enormous. Subjects covered include setting up a company for trading; timing the sale of shares; claiming expenses; dividends; negative gearing; managed funds; and record-keeping.

Many people who purchase a small business find it does not live up to their expectations – let alone the seller's optimistic forecasts. Some buyers suffer crippling losses when their new business fails completely, and yet most of these failures could have been avoided if only the purchasers had done their homework *before* buying. This invaluable book provides questions to ask to test the validity of information provided by the seller, as well as information on finding a suitable business; examining the finances; getting a fair price; options for structuring the business; and how to ensure there are no surprises after you take over.

Anyone who wants to set up as a private share trader has plenty of options. There is an array of 'off the peg' programs, plans, methods or systems to choose from. But do they work for just anyone? Tony Compton and Eric Kendall don't think so. They believe that all traders are different, and that a strategy or approach that works for one trader will not necessarily work for another. Every trader needs their own plan to profit from the

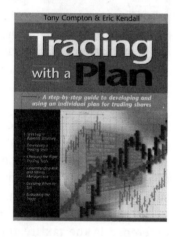

sharemarket. *Trading With a Plan* takes the reader step-by-step through the development of a 'tailor made' plan.